INDEX

ON CENSORSHIP

D1080901

Salima Ghezali

ANGELA ROBSON/AMNESTY INTERNATIONAL

INDEX ON CENSORSHIP 3 1996

Volume 25 No 3 May/June 1996   Issue 170

Index on Censorship (ISSN 0306-4220) is published bi-monthly by a non-profit-making company: Writers & Scholars International Ltd, Lancaster House, 33 Islington High Street, London N1 9LH

Tel: 0171-278 2313
Fax: 0171-278 1878
E-mail: indexoncenso@gn.apc.org
http://www.oneworld.org/index_oc/

Index on Censorship is associated with Writers & Scholars Educational Trust, registered charity number 325003
Second-class postage (US subscribers only) paid at Irvington, New Jersey. Postmaster: send US address changes to *Index on Censorship* c/o Virgin Mailing & Distribution, 10 Camptown Road, Irvington, NJ 07111

Subscriptions 1996 (6 issues p.a.)
Individuals: UK £36, US $50, rest of world £42

Institutions: UK £40, US $70, rest of world £46
Students: UK £25, US $35, rest of world £31

© This selection Writers & Scholars International Ltd, London 1996
© Contributors to this issue, except where otherwise indicated

Printed by Martins, Berwick upon Tweed, UK

Cover design by Andrea Purdie

EDITORIAL

Extremes of art and violence

WHAT kind of art is produced in the least censored country in the world? And what sort of society does this art portray? The critic Roger Kimball claims that both art and freedom have been trivialised in the USA by the drive to 'shock and discommode'. Is the new art of America the self-indulgence of the 'spoilt brats of western civilisation deprived of the revelations of necessity' that Ted Hughes once described? Or is it minority groups asserting their cultural rights, as Edward Lucie-Smith would claim? In investigating not so much censorship as the lack of it, *Index* asks some awkward questions about the connections between censorship, morality and aesthetics.

To the public, the suicide bombings by Hamas in Israel and the IRA's renewed campaign in London came as a surprise. Nur Masalha from Jerusalem and Mary Holland in Dublin argue that in neither case did the violence come out of the blue and that the press had their own reasons for not wanting to write about the danger signals — or even to see them. Meanwhile, as Peres recklessly attacks the Lebanon weeks before the election he hopes to win, it is hard not to conclude that violence in the Middle East has become a mark of credibility, a message to your own people that you are tough and they should trust you. It's the final cynicism — violence not as a way of finding a solution but as an aid to political survival.

The extraordinary comeback of Boris Yeltsin is an example of political survival which has yet to be put to the test. *Index* publishes a country file on the social and political condition of Russia before the June elections, where, according to Sergei Kovalev, 'the battle for power, for the hearts and minds of Russia's citizens, is not being fought between democratic forces on the one hand and totalitarian forces on the other, but between varying forms of the new totalitarianism.'

IN the last issue of *Index* we inadvertently left off the name of Ruthie Petrie, who compiled and edited, with her usual competence and panache, the feature on new censors in publishing — for which many apologies to her. ❏

contents

Index on Censorship **and Writers and Scholars Educational Trust** depend on
donations to guarantee their independence
and to fund research

The Trustees and Directors would like to thank all those whose
donations support *Index* and WSET, including

**Channel Four Television, Charity Know How,
The Goldberg Family Charitable Trust**

news in the

- **Poison pen** The Chinese army has slapped a ban on foreign penpals — because they 'contaminate soldiers' ideological purity and discipline'.

- **'Ear 'ear!** Iraq's human rights record looks set to improve, according to the Baghdad daily *al-Qadissiya*. Military deserters and others convicted of treason will no longer lose their ears to their leader, only 500,000 dinars to a cash-strapped regime and some months in 're-education' camps.

- **182 journalists** are in prison worldwide, says the Committee to Protect Journalists' annual report, released in March — a record (*see* Index *2/1996, page 188*).

- **Chernobyl-like secrecy** still surrounds information about Russia's environment, as Alexander Nikitin is finding out. Nikitin, a researcher for a Norwegian environmental group, is in prison on charges of espionage for his work on radioactive contamination in Murmansk.

- **Biting the hand...** International financier George Soros was publicly castigated as a 'CIA agent' shortly before his media foundation in Belgrade was closed down by Serbian authorities earlier this year. The Soros Yugoslavia Foundation had been supporting Serbia's few independent media, one of which, *Borba*, recently taken over by the government, published the accusation.

• **Netwatch** Thailand announces new measures to stop the spread of cyberporn — peddlers are now liable to charges of criminal defamation... Singapore describes new restrictions against porn and politics on the Net as 'an anti-pollution measure in cyberspace'... And in the USA, a government witness appearing in the American Civil Liberties Union's suit against the online decency law admits it's highly unlikely that the casual surfer will accidentally stumble on porn.

• **Bookwatch** After the furore that descended on Cambridge University Press when it dropped the book *Fields of Wheat, Rivers of Blood* (*Index* 2/1996) comes news that revisionist historian David Irving's US publisher has suddenly dropped his new biography of Goebbels. And in the UK, publishers John Wiley have done a U-turn on publishing *General Intelligence and its Implications*, by self-confessed 'scientific racist' Christopher Brand.

• **British values** Having been battered over journalist Bill Goodwin's right to protect his sources, and with a forthcoming ruling on blasphemy laws likely to go against them, the British government is not happy with the European Court of Human Rights. Ministers have been trying to paint the Court's rulings as an unwarranted interference in internal affairs.

Visual art is not protected by the First Amendment, says a New York judge. New York steet artists disagree, and are being arrested for selling their works on the sidewalks of SoHo without a licence

Right: Robert Lederman, president of ARTIST (Artists' Response to Illegal State Tactics), http://homepage.interaccess.com/~mar/nyc.html

• Radio Hope

BURUNDI has a new independent radio station, courtesy of the European Commission. Radio Amwizero (Radio Hope) is meant to counteract the effects of 'hate media' such as the hardline Hutu station Radio Democracy. 'We are taking steps to combat this station and journalists responsible have already been suspended from their jobs or imprisoned,' says communications minister Antoine Baza. Radio Democracy has recently been jammed by rock music broadcast over its transmission frequency, the source of which remains a mystery. Meanwhile, as we warned in our last issue, violence continues to escalate. The International Committee of the Red Cross confirmed on 4 April that more than 55,000 people had fled their homes since the start of March, when Hutu rebels launched a new offensive in the southwest.

• Double jeopardy

FIVE-AND-A-HALF years of UN sanctions have reduced Iraq to semi-starvation and set back Iraq's healthcare system by 50 years, says the latest report from the World Health Organisation. Released on 25 March, the report claims malaria, typhoid and cholera have reached epidemic levels and infant mortality has doubled.

Faced by a desperate and starving population, Saddam Hussein has made a policy U-turn and is discussing Resolution 986 — the 'Oil-for-Food' deal — with the UN. The Iraqi regime had previously rejected any such deal on the grounds that it violated national sovereignty.

Supporters of sanctions claim this as a sign that sanctions are working; that they are a more humane instrument of political change than military action. It is only a matter of time, they argue, before the current regime in Baghdad falls and the population's suffering is ended. Opponents of sanctions, backed by opposition groups in exile, dispute the weakness of the regime: with the culture of fear prevalent in Iraqi society, internal opposition destroyed, the general population too preoccupied with staying alive, too mindful of the brutal suppression of the post-war risings of Kurds and Iraqi Shia, to challenge the present ruler and his army, Saddam is likely to stay. On the contrary, argue opponents of sanctions, they have enabled Saddam to present himself as a martyr of western imperialism, strengthen his grip on a weak and divided population and wreak a terrible vengeance on his enemies in the south, the Marsh Arabs, whose environment and centuries-old lifestyle has been destroyed by the drainage of the marshes. The only effect of sanctions, argue these people, is the collective punishment of a people for the sins of its leader.

Officially, sanctions will not be lifted until Iraq complies with all UN resolutions demanding the destruction of its chemical and biological weapons programme. But given the West's ambivalence on the removal of Saddam while the country remains the one bulwark against the extension of Iran's interests in the region, sanctions were never intended to remove Saddam in the short term. Rather, to maintain the present regime and the country intact until a new leadership, more amenable to western interests, emerged from within.

Far from being the 'merciful alternative' urged by their supporters, sanctions have become the instrument with which the West, most notably the USA, seeks to reshape the future in the Gulf. They are as much a violation of the rights of the Iraqi people as the brutal tactics used by Saddam to silence and intimidate any internal challenge to his rule.

• When troubles come

IT TOOK an appeal court ruling and the rebuke of its presiding judge to persuade UK home secretary Michael Howard to withdraw his expulsion order on Saudi dissident Mohammed al-Mas'ari. This he did on 18 April, just within the month allowed by judge David Pearl for the implementation of his 'strong recommendation' that the home secretary reconsider the claim for asylum, which, added the judge, Michael Howard was not in any case entitled to refuse.

In a minor face-saving gesture, al-Mas'ari was not given the asylum he has been seeking, but 'exceptional leave to remain' — and to continue his campaign against the House of Saud — for four years. Tantamount, say immigration experts, to full asylum in all but name.

Despite the initial pressure it brought to bear on the British government to silence its most vociferous critic, the Saudi royal family professes itself satisfied with the outcome: the UK government failed, but not until it had pushed the law to the limits and beyond in an attempt to oblige its esteemed client.

But Saudi troubles with its dissidents in exile are not over. Not only is al-Mas'ari's Committee for the Defense of Legitimate Rights free to bombard the Kingdom with his 'scurrilous' faxes, a CDLR splinter group, the Movement for Islamic Reform led by former al-Mas'ari aide, Sa'ad al-Faqih, has set up a sophisticated hi-tech broadcasting studio on the outskirts of London from which he intends to beam in his anti-Saudi propaganda to the million or more semi-legal satellite dishes installed across Saudi Arabia. To circumvent recently proposed amendments in the British Broadcasting Bill forbidding direct transmissions to non-European states without a licence, al-Faqih's broadcasts will be relayed via Internet to continental Europe, and thence to the Kingdom. Al-Faqih, himself awaiting a ruling on his asylum application, is well aware of the narrow line he treads between Saudi displeasure and the British law. The British Broadcasting Corporation's decision to close its Arabic TV service in April after Saudi complaints, indicates that Michael Howard could again find himself under siege from Saudi sensibilities.

• Final verdict

THE Algerian League for the Defense of Human Rights (LADDH) has finally (April) published the full version of its Preliminary Report on the Massacre in Serkadji Prison on 21 February 1995 (*see page 180*). Its presentation was the occasion for a forthright condemnation of massive human rights violations by the government from LADDH's president, lawyer Ali Yahia Abdennour. 'Human rights are finished in this country,' he said. 'The mutilated and decapitated corpses picked up on our streets are the work of a government whose 'talk of human rights is no more than window-dressing for international consumption'.

The lawyer did not mince his words: 'This law demanding an eye for an eye is a travesty of our state law. It removes any shred of legality from the army's actions against the armed groups.' He added that information attributing many attacks to the GIA (Groupe Islamique Armé), and given massive media coverage, had been 'manipulated' by the security services as part of their 'anti-terrorist propaganda'.

He also deplored the fact that while thousands had died or been the victims of degrading and humiliating treatment, the international media was highly selective in its coverage of deaths. 'A mother's grief is the same whether her son has been killed by the police, the Islamists or any others.'

• Silence over Israel

IT TOOK the USA two days publicly to reprove Israel for its wanton attack on Lebanon and make some tentative move to defuse the situation. By then, it had silenced the voice of the UN by vetoing a vote of censure in the Security Council, there were 400,000 refugees on the roads of Lebanon fleeing combat zones, and hundreds dead as a result of an 'unfortunate mistake' — Israel's euphemism for its attack on a UN base in southern Lebanon.

It was left to former deputy secretary of state Richard Murphy, to 'regret' that his country had not reacted sooner and spared the Lebanon Israel's disproportionate use of force, as well as reigning in Shimon Peres before the peace process in which the US president has so much at stake, was finally — perhaps terminally — derailed.

But in the USA, no less than in Israel, an election looms. Clinton, as much as Peres, has reason to fear defeat. No time this for Clinton to risk alienating powerful democratic lobbies; time rather for Peres to prove his hawkish credentials to a credulous electorate and for Yasser Arafat, head of the Palestinian National Authority, to shake hands with Peres in a well publicised demonstration that it was business as usual on the peace process.

• Mirror, mirror...

THE UK Labour Party's principled support for government measures limiting cross-ownership of the media has run aground on its leader Tony Blair's unprincipled decision that this might no longer be in the interests of a party that, with the support of certain mass circulation dailies, could see its way clear to winning the next election.

Blair has been wooing media moguls like Rupert Murdoch, owner of *The Times* and the powerful tabloid, the *Sun*, both traditional supporters of the Tory vote with just this in mind.

His new target appears to be the Mirror Group, long-term supporter of the left in its mass-circulation tabloid the *Daily Mirror*, and now with a controlling influence in the liberal dailies the *Independent* and *Independent on Sunday*.

Under the proposed Broadcasting Bill, which sets the circulation threshold at 20 per cent of national newspaper circulation, the Mirror Group, along with Murdoch's News International, would be automatically precluded from merging with domestic television channels.

• Custodial sentence

EXCESSIVE secrecy and the absence of rules demanding the disclosure of information by police and prison authorities have contributed to the aura of suspicion surrounding deaths in custody in UK prisons and police stations. *Racial Discrimination and Deaths in Custody*, presented by the NGO INQUEST to the UN Committee for the Elimination of All Forms of Racial Discrimination (CERD) in March this year, details 24 deaths in custody between 1990 and 1995. Official statistics, excluding the London Metropolitan Police area of jurisdiction, give 123 deaths in police custody alone between 1991 and 1994.

Not all deaths occurred violently: the report produces evidence of medical neglect and lack of care of inmates who later committed suicide.

CERD 'strongly condemned' the UK government's lack of will to investigate and prosecute deaths in custody. INQUEST commented that 'the failure of the state to act...suggests that the victims are worthless and sends a clear message that these deaths don't matter'. ❏

• **To Urania: Selected Poems 1965-1985** *by Joseph Brodsky, from which the poem 'May 24 1980', printed in* Index *2/1996, was taken, is published in the USA by Farrar, Straus & Giroux*

ISABEL HILTON

The long arm of commerce

Faced with western competition for the lucrative China trade, human rights organisations are hard pressed to get their Chinese motion through the Geneva session of the UN Human Rights Commission

IN THE aftermath of the European Inter-Governmental Conference in Turin, Susanna Agnelli, the Italian foreign minister, indicated in her press conference that Europe's foreign ministers, in the course of a lunchtime discussion, had decided to support the USA in an attempt to pass a resolution criticising China in the United Nations Human Rights Commission session in Geneva at the end of April.

Such things have a way of sounding arcane. But the battle over this resolution has been hard fought and its outcome will send a signal of critical importance to China, in a year in which the People's Republic has tested to the limits the willingness of the world to turn a blind eye to its abuses.

Was it then a victory for the human rights lobby that Agnelli announced in Turin? Up to a point. But it has come late in the day. Unless the European Union now lobbies vigorously for the resolution, it may turn out, at best, a tactical stalemate between governments that have been mesmerised by the rapid growth of the Chinese economy and those who argue that if China is to become a regional, or even a global superpower, it is the more important that western governments now support the development of democracy and the protection of human rights.

It is an odd year in which to hesitate over such a resolution: it's only a matter of weeks since China's best-known dissident, Wei Jingsheng, was sentenced to a 14-year prison term, after a mockery of a trial and in the teeth of international protest, on the implausible charge of trying to overthrow the Chinese government; the air is only slowly cooling over the Taiwan Straits after China's ill-judged attempt to disrupt the first free presidential elections in Taiwan with a series of missile tests; and in the last few weeks, two human rights reports, one from Amnesty International (AI) and another from the Tibet Support Group and the Tibet Information Network, have forcefully echoed the conclusion of the earlier report from the US State Department — that the human rights situation in China has suffered a marked deterioration.

It has been a year of repression on many fronts: in Tibet there has been an escalation of the propaganda war against the exiled Dalai Lama that reached a crescendo over the dispute about the recognition of the eleventh Panchen Lama (*Index* 1/1996). The government in Beijing rejected the candidate the Dalai Lama had recognised, following the Dalai Lama's announcement in May 1995 and, after seven months of cracking the whip over a reluctant religious establishment, forced a lottery in which another boy was chosen. Since then, any protest has been suppressed and Tibetans have been warned that the first requirement of any religion is patriotism.

It's a message that has been given to the Muslims in Xinjiang, too, where, according to AI, a number of Muslim nationalists have been executed in recent years for alleged involvement in protests, underground political activities or bombings. Torture has become endemic and the use of administrative detention, often in labour camps, is a commonplace. There are still no legal safeguards against the abuse of state power and the state executes more people in China each year than do all the other countries of the world combined.

China, meanwhile, is enjoying the fruits of economic reform — unprecedented growth rates, a spectacular nationwide building boom and, for some, a rapid rise in living standards. With it come the problems — of pollution, of a widening gap between the rich and poor, the loss of agricultural land to building, and rising crime. The Communist Party, riddled with corruption and ideologically bankrupt, relies heavily on a mixture of repression and an appeal to nationalism to retain its grip on power. Within the Party itself, a handful of weak would-be leaders maintain an uneasy watch on each other around the moribund patriarch Deng Xiaoping. None of this bodes well for the prospects of a political liberalisation to accompany the economic liberalisation of the last 17 years.

But economic development does have political effects. At the international level, it has opened China to outside influences and the lines of communication with the outside can no longer simply be severed when they prove inconvenient. And more openness to trade profile brings the need for membership of international organisations that expect compliance with international norms. For the government in Beijing it poses the challenge of finding a place in the world acceptable both in Beijing and outside. It is a challenge China has so far failed.

In so far as Beijing's current posture is coherent, it consists of trying to reap the benefits of participation without paying the price of conforming to the rules. China is a permanent member of the Security Council of the United Nations and has adopted the Vienna Declaration and Programme of Action on Human Rights. Yet it consistently refuses to acknowledge that its treatment of its own citizens is anybody's business but its own. The problem for western governments is what to do about it.

It is not just the European Union that has hesitated over how best to tackle this problem. The USA, too, is grappling with conflicting policies. Crudely put, all China's trading partners are torn between the desire to profit from the China market and the moral (and legal) obligation to uphold international standards of behaviour. At a slightly more sophisticated level, the dilemma breaks down into the familiar opposition between the quiet diplomacy of engagement — which has the side benefit that business as usual can be maintained — and those who believe that the continued flaunting of international norms demands a more vigorous and public challenge.

For the USA, one watershed was reached two years ago when the Clinton administration de-linked Most Favoured Nation status and the question of human rights. Until then, MFN depended on the annual certification by Congress of continued progress in human rights. But the Clinton administration argued that de-linking would bring increased goodwill to the relationship which would allow the USA to exert a continued pressure in favour of human rights — more effective, they argued, than public rebuke. And as a tacit quid pro quo, the US also began to support the European Union in sponsoring a resolution against China in Geneva, should the need arise.

The need has not been lacking since but, so far, no resolution has been passed. The first attempts were sidetracked and never reached a vote. Last year, to the astonishment of many human rights monitors, it not only came to a vote but was also only defeated by a single vote when Russia switched sides at the last moment and voted with China.

The importance of the issue to China can be gauged by the degree of effort it puts into avoiding criticism. Many human rights activists have been imprisoned, Beijing has permitted no International Commission of the Red Cross (ICRC) inspection and AI is regularly condemned as part of a global plot against China.

The harassment of AI has lately taken on an international aspect. When it launched its latest China report in March in Bangkok and, a few days later in Nepal, the local police took a vigorous interest in the proceedings. In Nepal, some 200 human rights and Tibetan refugees were arrested as they embarked on a peace march to the Chinese embassy to mark the launch of the AI report. The government in Kathmandu explained the arrests by saying that it would not 'permit its soil to be used against its neighbour'.

Western governments cannot be so overtly intimidated, but behind the scenes, both governments and businessmen are told in firm terms that any act considered 'unfriendly' to China will have serious consequences when contracts are handed out. Such threats have had their effect: human rights monitors have complained that there has been a marked effort to turn down the level of attention the European Union pays to human rights since Sir Leon Brittan took over the task of formulating the Commission's policy towards China and some human rights groups believe that the difficulties they have experienced with negotiating funding from the Commission are related to Chinese pressure. And this year several leading member states have come under pressure over the question of the resolution in Geneva.

In March 1995, the US State Department's annual human rights report contained a particularly bleak assessment of the success to date of constructive engagement: economic liberalisation in China had not brought political reform: in fact, in human rights terms, the plight of one billion Chinese citizens had worsened. The US had sacrificed its ability to influence Beijing's behaviour by severing the link between human rights practices and preferential trading and had been rewarded, as the report said, with the following results: 'Overall, in 1995 the authorities stepped up repression of dissent. By year's end, almost all public dissent against the central authorities was silenced by intimidation, exile or imposition of prison terms.' And had the trade balance benefited as a result?

Unfortunately not. Though the overall volume of trade had risen, so had the negative balance. Perhaps spurred on by the knowledge of what their own report would say, the US State Department resolved to commit considerable effort to getting a resolution through in Geneva.

On 19 February this year, the USA and the European Union met to co-ordinate their approach. It was agreed that a resolution would be tabled, though the text was not agreed. That meeting was followed by a EU working group meeting on 28 February at which an understanding was also reached that the EU would support a resolution. But by early March, when the EU ambassadors met in Rome with Chinese representatives, the position had slipped: it was decided there to postpone the final decision on sponsoring a resolution until the foreign ministers met at the end of the month in Brussels. China, meanwhile, was to be given notice that the EU would back a resolution unless Beijing responded positively and convincingly to EU concerns.

WHAT had happened in the meantime? European leaders had been busy in the Far East. They had attended the first ever Asia-Europe summit and many had taken advantage of the trip to chat to the Chinese about business. Among the glittering promises held out by the Chinese is the chance for the Airbus consortium — of which British, French, German and Spanish companies are members — to sell both wide and narrow bodied passenger aircraft, worth in excess of US$2 billion in contracts, to China. President Chirac held talks in Bangkok with Chinese premier Li Peng and reports in the French media claim progress was made. Human rights were not high on the Bangkok agenda. And, by a curious coincidence, France has been lobbying strenuously against the Geneva resolution.

Airbus has only seven per cent of the Chinese market and is keen to enlarge its market share. The first indication that Airbus might prevail against the US company Boeing in the forthcoming purchases came in March when the Chinese trade minister, Wu Yi, postponed a trip to Washington after the Clinton administration threatened to take action against China for another violation of international norms — the continuing failure to deal with the wholesale infringement of intellectual property rights. As the USA fell into disfavour, France's star began to rise. During Li Peng's April visit to France, the premier committed China to future Airbus purchases worth US$1.7 billion, though the sale of only 10

Airbus 320s was confirmed at the time: something of a disappointment for French manufacturers, reported *Le Monde*.

The US is wrestling with its own dilemma: Congress is in a highly charged state about China and is unlikely to grant a renewal of Most Favoured Nation status in June without some gesture of disapproval. For the United States, that means Geneva. In Washington, the realisation that France was lobbying against the resolution was particularly unwelcome. Not only did it threaten to deprive the administration of its peace offering for Congress, but, since the EU decision to co-sponsor the resolution is taken by consensus, France's resistance threatened to leave the US isolated. Under such circumstances, the US would be forced to drop it.

According to human rights groups, the irony is that, provided western nations maintain their unity, there is little to fear from Chinese threats. When the German Parliament held hearings on Tibet last year, it was against a background of furious protests from Beijing. But the hearings went ahead and German trade has not suffered. If the Chinese tactic of creating splits between western governments is seen to succeed, the threats will be used to greater effect.

The threat of a resolution in Geneva has already produced a flurry of activity in the Chinese National People's Congress. On 7 April, it passed a law giving suspects the hitherto unheard of privilege of being treated as innocent until proven guilty. The NPC also reduced the legal length of detention without an arrest warrant from several months to 30 days. The first measure has brought China into line with UN requirements, implying that UN standards on torture and criminal process could be productive leverage points if western countries were prepared to be robust.

So whose victory was it in Turin? On the surface, France has been brought back into line. But the delay caused by France's foot-dragging has lost the resolution's sponsors valuable lobbying time. The UN Human Rights Commission, which has a rotating membership, is a less liberal body this year than last. In Turin, Susanna Agnelli acknowledged that the EU had held off sponsoring the resolution in the hope that quiet diplomacy would produce a result. It failed. Now it may be too late, this year at least, for a noisier approach. ❑

Isabel Hilton *is a writer and broadcaster. She is currently writing a book on the Panchen Lama*

NUR MASALHA

Jerusalem 1996

A different peace

It was not only the bombs that derailed the Middle East peace
process. Even before then, the omissions of the Oslo Accords,
the refusal to talk to Hamas when the chance offered and the
reluctance of Israel to treat on the hard questions, had slowed
down negotiations on a peace many Palestinians felt left them
worse off than ever. Now, Shimon Peres's brutal bombardment of
Lebanon has removed peace from the domestic agenda. It may
have improved Peres's credibility with the Israeli electorate; it
also risks driving more Palestinians into the arms of Hamas

THE latest spate of suicide bombings that claimed some 60 Israeli lives was terrorism at its most savage: cruel and indiscriminate assaults on targets that cannot be justified — not by the memory of the Hebron massacre, not by the Israeli Shin Bet's 'legally sanctioned' torture of Palestinian prisoners, not even by Israel's appalling record of nearly three decades of occupation.

Yet it is not difficult to see who is most damaged by them: the Palestinian National Authority (PNA), headed by Yasser Arafat, and the inhabitants of the West Bank and the Gaza Strip.

In the fevered aftermath of the outrages, the Israeli Labour government imposed an indefinite blockade on the West Bank and Gaza, more severe than in the darkest days of the Likud government. Shortages of food and medicines are acute; several Palestinians — including two newly born babies — who needed urgent medical attention died while ambulances carrying them were held for hours at Israeli army roadblocks.

For many Israelis, the renewal of violence by the Islamists, after the diplomatic breakthroughs in the Palestinian-Israeli negotiations, was a source of bitter anger and disillusionment. There is bound to be a swing against any substantial concessions. The same outrages will also imperil the electoral prospects of prime minister Shimon Peres on 29 May. Like Arafat, he is anxious to keep negotiations going. Within the Israeli establishment the temptation to return to the 'iron fist' attitudes of the past has been difficult to resist. Sadly, however, the very 'security' methods Peres is currently adopting on an unprecedented scale — and forcing Arafat to adopt against his own people — are threatening to derail the whole peace process. By inflicting severe hardship on two million people, by flooding the West Bank roads with army patrols and checkpoints, by its heavy-handed crackdown — the curfews, the searches, the daily humiliation, the home sealing and demolition, the closing of schools and colleges — Peres risks driving even more Palestinians into the militant camp.

Most Israelis are either unwilling or unable to comprehend the fact that the latest wave of suicidal violence has not come out of the blue; that one doesn't have to be a supporter of Hamas or, still worse, the Islamic Jihad to see how Palestinian rights have been blocked or put in limbo by the negotiations process. Most Palestinians supported the Declaration of Principles (the Oslo Accords of September 1993), in the hope that it would constitute the first step towards dismantling the occupation in the

West Bank and the Gaza Strip. But since then, the Oslo track has turned out to be terribly unjust.

Dictated by the stronger party, Israel, the various agreements signed since Oslo have never been based on equitable coexistence. Three years down the Oslo route, all the Palestinian people has been offered is administrative autonomy in 65 per cent of the Gaza Strip (less than five per cent of historic Palestine) and in several splintered patches of West Bank territory, without freedom of movement, sovereignty or territorial integrity. On every crucial issue — land, settlements, water, sovereignty, Jerusalem, borders, refugees — Palestinian rights have yet to be addressed.

Nearly 60 per cent of the Palestinians — mostly refugees who were expelled from their ancestral lands in 1948 — are still living in exile, hundreds of thousands of them rotting in miserable refugee camps. They have been excluded from Shimon Peres's vision of a new and peaceful Middle East. Is it unnatural that they feel the peace on offer is not worth having? It is no coincidence, more a reflection of their anger at exclusion from the peace process, that three out of the four suicide bombers lived in the squalor of refugee camps: two in the al-Fawwar refugee camp on the outskirts of occupied Hebron, the third in the Khan Yunis refugee camp, surrounded by the bleak daily reality of life in the Gaza Strip.

Directly or indirectly, the Palestinians are still under the Israeli thumb. In the West Bank Israel is determined to consolidate its settler colonialism. Withdrawal from this territory has, in practice, become 'redeployment': Israeli settlement activity has continued as openly as before; confiscation of Arab lands to build new bypass roads for the nearly 150 settlements has been speeded up in recent months. It is safe to assume that the large settlements established at the heart of the West Bank — such as Maalei Adumim, Ariel and Kiryat Arba — were built to stay. Their size and infrastructure have been considerably expanded since the Oslo Accords were signed and their illegal existence will almost certainly be legitimised by the negotiations process. The large Jewish settlements in and around East Jerusalem were also built to stay. Going from Bethlehem to Ramallah (both towns are under the PNA) involves a long and dangerous journey around the unilaterally annexed and sealed off city of Arab Jerusalem. Palestinians here live in isolation from the rest of the West Bank and face an uncertain future.

No less important is the fact that the Islamist suicidal attacks are an integral part of a pattern of violence that Israel itself has done much to create. Its reprisal raids, bombing of refugee camps, 1982 invasion of Lebanon and siege of Beirut which cost some 20,000 Palestinian and Lebanese lives, its 'bone-breaking' and 'iron fist' methods of dealing with the intifada, in which around 2,000 Palestinians died, as well as its assassinations of Palestinian leaders like Hamas' Yahia Ayyash, alias the Engineer, or Islamic Jihad's Dr Fathi Shqaqi, have all kept the endless circle of violence going.

By giving the order to assassinate the Engineer in January, Peres was partly responsible for breaking the de facto ceasefire which had been kept by the Islamists for months. He must, by now, be aware of the extreme difficulty of foiling the would-be 'martyrs' who are prepared to commit suicide and against whom there is little real deterrent. His declaration of a 'total war' on Hamas, while ignoring the underlying causes of its violence, will almost certainly be counter-productive. Suspending or slowing down the negotiations, putting two million people under siege, arresting and torturing still more, will only aggravate Palestinian resentment, providing fertile ground for more violent protest, more 'martyrdoms'.

Palestinians, all but a fraction of whom are opposed to the Islamists' terror strikes, can no more tolerate indefinite closure of the Occupied Territories than the Israelis can the suicide outrages that feed on the poverty and degradation which the closure serves only to worsen.

As long as Israel continues its repression and the economic hardship of the Palestinian masses worsens, the negotiations process will remain a shambles, the Palestinians will remain divided and the PNA will remain weak and dominated by Israel. The resulting vacuum will be occupied by Hamas and other still more militant organisations.

Dialogue with the political leadership of Hamas, which in the past proved to be remarkably pragmatic, and an effort to restore the ceasefire while addressing the social and economic problems that continue to drive people to support the militant Islamists, is more likely to contribute towards breaking the cycle. Simultaneously, the negotiations process should be put on a more just footing and expedited.

Palestinians do want an end to the violence. But they also dream of a different kind of peace based on non-domination and equitable coexistence, with self-determination for both peoples, each with equal national rights and expectations. ❑

Nur Masalha *is a Palestinian academic from the Galilee, Israel*

SHOSHANA BERI-EICHOUNI

Israel must speak to Hamas

AFTER the appalling bombings in Jerusalem and Tel Aviv, the desire for revenge is uppermost among Israelis. It was no different on the other side after the assassination of Yahia Ayyash, alias the 'Engineer' and bombmaker extraordinaire to Hamas, killed by the Israeli secret services. It was his mother who demanded that before they could get on with the business of peace, his death must first be avenged. Common sense tells us that we have to break this vicious cycle of revenge.

The truce lasted over six months and ended only with the assassination of Ayyash. It demonstrated that Arafat and Hamas were both capable of being brought into the peace process. Israel's persistent refusal to listen to Hamas' demands has led to an increasingly bloody conflict. More than 18 months ago, in October 1994, the movement's leadership was ready to join in the process. When elections in the Occupied Territories were discussed at the Cairo conference, Hamas declared itself willing to take part. Israel, however, made it clear that this could only be on one condition: that Hamas accept the Oslo Accords and renounce its stated intention of destroying the state of Israel. In other words, Israel attempted to impose conditions it had not demanded of its partners in Oslo: Fatah [PLO] has still not abrogated the clause in its charter specifying the overthrow of Israel and half the population is still opposed to the Oslo Accords.

Instead of leaving the Palestinians to organise elections as they wished, with representatives of their own choice, Israel insisted that Hamas be sidelined. Yet, right up to the very moment of Arafat's return, they had regarded him as the very soul of the intifada.

Hamas is not simply a paramilitary grouping. It is primarily a political organisation that runs a wide range of civilian community projects throughout the territories. It was a mistake at the time, as it is now, to

Life in Gaza 1995: a breeding ground for Hamas

imagine that Hamas would give up its role and influence without acknowledgement of its rightful place in that society. The fight for that recognition was not long in coming: the attack on Nahalat Chiv'a in Jerusalem was followed some days later, in October 1994, by the kidnapping of Nachshon Waxman, a corporal in the Israeli army. Having failed to secure the release of their leader Sheik Yassin — one of their demands in exchange for Waxman's release — his kidnappers executed him.

It is evident from an examination of the Islamists' activities at that time, that Waxman's kidnapping was aimed at getting Israel to recognise Hamas as an important factor in the peace process. Informal contacts with Hamas had already taken place through Rabbi Frauman and the Arab-Israeli deputy, Al Sana, and there was some ground for hope. What Frauman said then remains true today: 'Just as we shall never have peace unless we have some understanding of the Jewish religious group, so, if we really want a peace agreement, we must secure at least a minimum of co-operation from the main Islamic group.'

Hamas was willing to extend the deadline on Waxman's execution; earlier they would have been satisfied simply with the release of Sheik Yassin, something Israel had already envisaged. But Israel determined to liberate Waxman by force and the military option won out over alternative methods.

The chance of dialogue with Hamas was thrown away. Once again, its response was swift. Terrorism escalated to a degree we had never experienced: the bus bomb on route number five in Jerusalem on 19 October 1994 that killed 22 people; followed by the bombs in Beit Lid, Ramat Gan and in bus number 26 in Jerusalem. These attacks will continue until Arafat realises that Hamas cannot be excluded from peace negotiations. The murder of Ayyash on 5 January 1996, however understandable from a military perspective, is out of tune with the times.

Whatever it costs us, I believe we have no other alternative but to try and speak with Hamas, or at least allow Arafat to bring it into the peace process. It is up to us to encourage those elements who are willing to enter into dialogue. Hamas is not a monolith. We must distinguish between political and military groupings, between Hamas in Gaza and the West Bank, and Hamas in, for instance, Syria.

Our differences and disputes with the Islamist movement are no different from those we previously had with Arafat and Fatah. Today, Hamas' conditions for peace, as well as its understanding of that peace, are unacceptable. There was a time when Arafat's demands and statements seemed equally beyond the pale. We could get a dialogue going by discussing anything whatsoever just as long as it did not threaten Israel's security. It is vital that those in both camps who support the Oslo Accords start working together to defeat all those in the opposing camp. ❏

Shoshana Beri-Eichouni is an Israeli historian. This article was first published in Ha'aretz, Tel Aviv

Translated by Judith Vidal-Hall

MARY HOLLAND

Why we should have known

The renewed IRA bombing campaign should have come as no surprise, argues one of Ireland's leading columnists. The media were in a position to know, but failed to warn the public

WHY did the breakdown of the Provisional IRA's ceasefire take everybody by surprise? Since the first bomb exploded near Canary Wharf, London, in February one question has been put over and over again to journalists: why was there no warning in the media that the situation had deteriorated to this extent?

To be fair, it does seem that even Sinn Fein leaders like Gerry Adams and Martin McGuinness did not know that the bomb was going to go off when it did. But equally, looking back now, it is clear that they did expect that, sooner or later, the IRA would lose patience with the slow pace of the peace process and that when this happened, its most likely target would be one of several prestige buildings in the City of London.

It's always been an article of faith that these 'spectaculars' in Britain have much more impact on politicians at Westminster than any number of deaths in Northern Ireland. 'When I saw John Major speaking in the House of Commons and "binning" the Mitchell Report (containing the recommendations of an international body set up under former US Senator George Mitchell to resolve the long-standing problem of decommissioning IRA weapons) I knew it was only a matter of time before the IRA did something,' one Sinn Fein member who had been an active supporter of the peace process told me.

It is ironic, all the same, that the original IRA ceasefire, announced at a time when Sinn Fein was still banned from the airwaves in Britain, was fully flagged in advance in the media. The return to violence took place when there was no official censorship of this kind, and Gerry Adams had a degree of access to the airwaves many politicians envied.

So how did we get it so wrong? Journalists — and I'm as much to blame as anyone — should have realised and reported that the situation was deteriorating fast, that a breakdown of the ceasefire could happen at any time. Whenever one talked to Gerry Adams, and those close to him in Sinn Fein, they warned of the growing impatience among Republican activists, that the pursuit of politics as an alternative to 'the armed struggle' was not yielding the tangible results they had expected — and which, they believed, they had been promised.

Within the IRA, where mistrust of the British government's motives and strategy in regard to Northern Ireland is deeply engrained, the suspicion was growing that they 'had been taken for a ride'. Those opposed to the 'alternative unarmed strategy' (ie politics) from the start had always argued that the British would raise obstacles to delay progress towards meaningful talks, and would then use that time to demoralise and break the IRA.

These tensions were reported but, for a whole variety of reasons, the real threat was not taken seriously. When Gerry Adams warned that the whole peace process could unravel he was accused by politicians of making threats or crying wolf. This disapproval was echoed by interviewers on television and in the editorial columns of most newspapers. By the time the ceasefire broke down he seemed to find it difficult to ward off these criticisms. I remember asking him what he meant when he said that the process could go 'into reverse' and his answer was to point his right hand upwards and, slowly, make a gesture as though pulling a trigger.

There were other warning signs which were reported but not, perhaps, properly analysed or understood. The increase in punishment shootings and beatings of alleged drug dealers were written about in terms of their savagery. The British and Irish governments insisted that, because they were not directed against members of the security forces, they did not constitute a breach of the ceasefire and journalists went along with this explanation. But what these attacks were about politically was that the IRA was determined to assert control of the ghetto areas from which it had traditionally drawn support. After the ceasefire was announced in 1994, many of these activists had become involved in political activity, organising marches and so on. They had been prepared, at the minimum, to give politics a chance. But even that level of support, according to Sinn

Fein, had been dropping away for some time before the Canary Wharf bomb. Politics, it seemed, was no longer credible.

There are many forms of censorship and, from personal experience, I know that self-censorship by journalists of what they write and report is the most corrosive, at least in a democracy where theoretically there are few restrictions on the freedom of the press. One saw this over and over again in Northern Ireland. Most journalists who reported on the conflict came to understand that they were working within serious, if unspoken, constraints — political disapproval, fear of offending public opinion, the denial of access to certain sources. To deny these realities, to insist on making waves, meant running the risk of being branded as 'unreliable', a 'Provo-lover', labels unlikely to help the individual's career prospects.

What this meant was that the public was not given the information to enable it to understand what was happening in Northern Ireland. Instead it was told that the IRA was a bunch of psychopaths, that it had no support in the Catholic community, that by drawing peace-loving people on both sides together the terrorists could be marginalised and defeated. To take an example: it was only after the leaking of an official British Army report which argued that the IRA could not be defeated by military methods that it became acceptable for journalists to voice the same views.

In the case of the ceasefire, different political influences were at work. Different but perhaps even more persuasive. After 17 months of peace we had come to believe that it could not break down. Those of us who had covered the tragedy of the Northern Ireland conflict for more than 20 years, stood in bleak graveyards, and watched the bewildered faces of widows and children, desperately wanted the peace to be secured. We seized on reasons for optimism, the enormous outpouring of emotion that greeted President Clinton's visit to Northern Ireland, for example. We either did not see, or did not want to see, the danger signals.

Worse still, there was considerable disapproval of those journalists who did go against the grain, insisted on reporting that tensions were growing within the Republican movement and that the peace could break down. There was a sense that they were somehow not fully committed to peace just as, in the past, there was an unspoken feeling that anyone who was critical of the police or the security forces was 'soft on terrorism'. ❏

Mary Holland *is a columnist with the* Irish Times, *Dublin*

OPINION

MARK FISHER

A little knowledge is a useful thing

Freedom of Information Acts cannot force governments to behave; they can and do lead to better decision-making and restore trust between the public and politicians

I F THERE had been a Freedom of Information Act on the UK statute book, would the British people have been better informed about Arms to Iraq or Bovine Spongiform Encephalopathy (BSE)? Would they have been spared the shambles of the Matrix Churchill affair, the trial, the Scott inquiry and the waste of an estimated £25 million (US$37.5 million) of taxpayers' money? Would the advice of scientific experts on BSE have been published and, if so, would it have averted the panic which has gripped both government and the public? Might, ironically, such an act, which the Thatcher and Major governments have resisted with such stubborn determination, have saved the Tories from the humiliation and ridicule of the Scott Report and the political mess of BSE?

Support for a substantial Freedom of Information Act has been growing steadily for more than 10 years, led by Maurice Frankel's Campaign for Freedom of Information and by the work of Charter 88 and others, including *Index on Censorship*. By the time the Right to Know Bill was debated by Parliament in 1993 and two attempts had been made by Tony Wright MP and then by Don Touhig MP to get a Whistleblowers' Bill passed in 1995 and 1996, virtually every commentator and national newspaper accepted that freedom of information legislation was a key element in constitutional and democratic reform; that it would open up not just Whitehall and the political system, but the way in which our society operated; and might even begin to restore a sliver of confidence in politicians.

However there is a danger that, having wished so long for a Freedom of Information Act, we have invested it with magic powers far beyond what it can realistically deliver. The Arms to Iraq and BSE affairs offer us concrete and practical yardsticks against which to test its possible effectiveness.

To gauge that efficacy, we need to ask some simple questions. Would a Freedom of Information Act, based on an amalgam of the Right to Know Bill and the Whistleblowers' Bill have brought to light and prevented the secret arms deals with Iraq which were in breach of the government's original guidelines? Would it have alerted Parliament to the policy change which altered those guidelines? Would it have avoided the prosecution of the Matrix Churchill directors?

On BSE, would a Freedom of Information Act have forced the government to share with the public the expert advice they had received and, if so, would we have been better informed in practice, and would such information have allayed or aggravated public anxieties?

Any substantial Freedom of Information Act is based on a presumption, described in Clause 1 of the 1993 Right to Know Bill, that the public has a right 'to obtain access information held by public authorities'. However, this right is always qualified by certain specific exemptions. In the two most recent generations of legislation, drafted by the national governments of Australia, Canada and New Zealand in the 1980s and by the states of Australia and provinces of Canada in the 1990s, these exemptions invariably cover material which could endanger defence, security and international relations; the enforcement of the law; personal privacy; the policy advice that ministers receive from civil servants; and commercial confidentiality. It is how these exemptions are drafted and, crucially, how refusals to disclose by government are reviewed and adjudicated, that determines the real effectiveness of freedom of information legislation.

Had legislation similar to the Right to Know Bill been law at the time of the Arms to Iraq affair, a simple application could have been made to the Department of Trade and Industry (DTI) requesting the publication of details of all export licences granted. It is likely that the DTI would have refused this application, claiming that disclosure fell outside the Act on a number of grounds: that it 'could reasonably be expected to cause damage to the interests of the United Kingdom in the conduct of international relations' (Right to Know Bill, Clause 19), and/or that it would 'be likely to cause significant damage to the lawful commercial or professional activities of a third party', in this case Matrix Churchill (Clause 24).

At that point the applicant, for instance a journalist or an MP, would ask for an internal review by the DTI and if, after 14 days, disclosure was still refused, could appeal to the information commissioner and tribunal who would have the power to call for all relevant public records and whose decision would have the force of a court order. In the case of the licences issued to Matrix Churchill, the commissioner and the tribunal would have had to balance the public interest and right to know against the right of the company to commercial confidentiality and would probably have ruled in favour of disclosure.

However, the disclosure of the policy changes by foreign office ministers presents different tests of a Freedom of Information Act. Here, to protect the workings of government, a Freedom of Information Act would exempt information about 'the formation of policy' and the records of 'any deliberation or decision of the Cabinet or of a Cabinet Committee'. However, this exemption would not cover factual information nor 'expert advice on a scientific, technical, medical, financial, statistical or legal matter' nor 'a guideline' (Clause 21).

The tribunal would have had to determine whether what were changed were the guidelines (if so, disclose), or the policy advice of civil servants (if so, exempt). A likely outcome would have been that any letters from ministers such as William Waldegrave expressing the change of government approach would be disclosable, but that any memorandum from a civil servant advising this or putting the case for and against such changes would be exempted.

A similar balance would apply to BSE. The government have been commissioning and receiving research from its expert scientific and medical advisers on this for 10 years, but, to date, none of that information has been disclosed to the public. Even after the issue erupted into the parliamentary and public arena in March, the only document available for public scrutiny, deposited in the library of the House of Commons, is a three-page statement, devoid of data from the Spongiform Encephalopathy Advisory Committee (SEAC).

Consequently it is impossible for journalists or scientists and doctors not involved in government, to come to any informed evaluation of whether ministers are making reasonable decisions. Once again in the absence of the facts, public debate is being conducted on the basis of assertion, counter-assertion and speculation. It is small wonder that debate of this scrawny quality fuels the public anxiety and uncertainty which is at the heart of the BSE issue.

These are precisely the circumstances where the publication of all the data on which the government is forming its judgements could make a real political contribution, and an application for disclosure under a Freedom of Information Act would almost certainly be upheld by an information tribunal on the basis that this was 'expert advice on a scientific, technical, medical...media' rather than exempt 'policy advice' (both Right to Know Bill, Clause 21).

So, much of the information at the heart of the Arms to Iraq and BSE affairs would, on balance, be likely to be published under a Freedom of Information Act provided that the existence of the information was known and that the appeals tribunal regime was strong and was independent of ministers.

Memoranda, data, research papers may be buried in the departmental recesses of Whitehall, often unknown to other departments, their existence revealed only by civil servants who are principled and brave enough to whistleblow in the knowledge that such actions will almost certainly end their careers. In these circumstances a measure of protection, such as would be provided by Tony Wright's and Don Touhig's Whistleblowers' Bill, is an essential element of a Freedom of Information Act.

More crucial still is the type of appeals mechanism and the powers of a commissioner and tribunal. In Australia, the tribunal is independent and judicial, having the power to order disclosure. In Canada the commissioner's role is conciliatory, negotiating the release of contentious information from government departments. Such differences of implementation finally determine the effectiveness of Freedom of Information Acts.

No Freedom of Information Act can prevent a government from acting badly or covertly, nor can it force disclosure. It simply provides a legal framework within which disclosure is possible. So, finally, the reality of a more open style of government returns, not to legislation itself, but to the political will and enthusiasm of any government to operate freedom of information legislation. If a government feels threatened by being open and implements freedom of information legislation reluctantly or cautiously, little will change. What we need is a government which believes that in the long term freedom of information will lead to better decision making and a climate of greater trust between the public and politicians.

More crucially, we need media, a general public, and individual civil servants and politicians who are determined to achieve more openness. Only then will government begin to treat the public not as children, whose little minds should not be bothered by, or trusted with, information, but as equal and adult partners in the process of government. ❏

Mark Fisher is Labour MP for Stoke-on-Trent Central. He introduced the Right to Know Bill in the House of Commons in 1993

MICHAEL FOLEY

The end of a heritage

The Republic of Ireland sheds its culture of secrecy, but journalists fear they will be left out in the cold

IT WAS probably the most prophetic sentence of the thousands uttered at the Beef Tribunal. The tribunal had been running seven months when the chairman, Justice Liam Hamilton, told politicians, beef industry people, journalists and lawyers: 'I think that if the questions that were asked in the Dail (Irish Parliament) were answered in the way they are answered here, there would be no necessity for this inquiry and a lot of money and time would have been saved.'

That was in January 1992. Justice Hamilton was not to know that the tribunal would carry on hearing evidence until June 1993 and would not report until August 1994. The IR£35 million (US$55 million) Tribunal of Enquiry into the Beef Industry was the longest, most expensive and controversial inquiry in the history of the Republic. It caused a general election; gave rise to three Supreme Court cases; led to an investigation by a parliamentary committee and a disciplinary hearing of the Bar Council; and it changed Irish politics — probably for ever.

Even those who did not understand the evidence about export credit insurance, EC rules and regulations governing the beef industry or had no comprehension about a beef industry subculture, did understand that they were looking at the workings of government and the relationship between politics and business for the first time. It was a rare glimpse into the secret workings of the state.

In 1993, a new coalition government was formed by Fianna Fail and Labour. One of the commitments in its Programme for Government echoed those words of Justice Hamilton, a promise of freedom of information legislation. To understand the enormity of such a promise it must be emphasised that the Irish state is one of the most secretive states in Europe, possibly even more so than the UK. The Irish version of the Official Secrets Act is not only an inheritance from a colonial past, but was tightened up in 1962 by the then Fianna Fail government who amended the act to give government ministers the final say on whether information is secret or not.

In essence, the Irish state operates on the basis that all official information is presumed secret unless otherwise stated. This means, ludicrously, that even the menu in the restaurant in the Irish Parliament is officially a secret document.

The Official Secrets Act, however, is only one factor within the range of instruments ensuring secrecy. Even the guarantee of freedom of the press in the constitution is heavily circumscribed by considerations of public order, morality and the authority of the state. Media law lecturer Marie McGonagle of University College, Galway, wrote in the *Irish Reporter* in 1992 of legislation relating to free speech as being a 'complex web' that was in need of urgent reform.

Journalists in Ireland joke about the government spokesman who is supposed to have said 'no comment and don't quote me'. They publish second-rate information as if it was the Watergate tapes because it is secret. In a rational world such information would probably not deserve publication at all, but in Ireland, where everything is secret, that fact alone warrants that it be put into the public domain. And when this takes place, the government orders an internal inquiry to find the leak.

The new government formed in 1994 after the collapse of the Labour/Fianna Fail coalition — partly because of the tensions caused when the report of the tribunal was published — also committed itself to freedom of information. The same junior minister, Eithne Fitzgerald, was left in charge of preparing the legislation in the new government.

As the fallout of the Beef Tribunal and the events that led to it continue to bedevil the Irish state, Fitzgerald has got Cabinet approval for her proposed legislation. What Irish MPs will be discussing is a Bill based on best practice from around the world, but mainly from New Zealand and Australia. It will give a statutory right of access to information held by government departments and public bodies, while the Ombudsman, as Information Commissioner, will safeguard the individual and public interest.

> The assumption that everything is secret unless otherwise declared, will be reversed. It will be illegal to withhold information unless it falls within a number of exceptions

There is a feeling that the minister has been forced to compromise in order to steer her legislation through. There has been disappointment over the 'whistleblowers' protection. In the Irish legislation civil servants aware of a wrongdoing can blow the whistle to authorities such as the Comptroller and Auditor General, or the police, but not to the press, nor to politicians, if they wish to ensure they are protected. There is also the vexed issue of Cabinet confidentiality which the Supreme Court ruled on during the Beef Tribunal. Some journalists believe the Bill will give even greater confidentiality to government than that awarded by the Supreme Court.

It was never going to be easy for Fitzgerald. The former Taoiseach (prime minister), Albert Reynolds, and the present Taoiseach, John Bruton, have been obsessively secret. Reynolds might state that he wanted to 'let in the light' on government and Bruton might have wished to conduct government business as if 'behind a pane of glass', but both men have never allowed such public utterances to interfere with doing business behind closed doors. Reynolds gave up a weekly on-the-record briefing session for journalists after only a few weeks, while the current government has been accused by one political writer of being the 'most closed and least transparent administration for more than 20 years'.

But now there is no going back. The government has committed itself to freedom of information; the main opposition party itself also committed itself when it was in government and now, rather than being seen to oppose freedom of information, is saying that the bill, as approved by the Cabinet, does not go far enough.

What Eithne Fitzgerald has done is genuinely radical. With luck, by this time next year, Irish citizens will have access to information as a right. They will be able to hold politicians accountable for decisions made, they will see how decisions are taken and have a right to information about themselves. Citizens will know how decisions affecting their lives in the most intimate way are taken and what information is being used to arrive at decisions affecting social welfare payments, tax levels or medical payments.

The assumption that everything is secret unless otherwise declared, will be reversed. It will be illegal to withhold information unless it falls within a number of exemptions.

The day the president signs into law the Freedom of Information Act — most likely later this year — will begin the change from a culture of secrecy to one of openness. If the government also has the confidence to hold a referendum on Cabinet confidentiality, change the laws of contempt of court (allowing journalists to protect their sources) and abolish the Official Secrets Act, then we may be confident that never again will it be necessary to hold an inquiry such as the Beef Tribunal in order to squeeze out the truth. ❏

Michael Foley *is media correspondent with the* Irish Times

Russia: Future imperfective

A pre-election report compiled by Irena Maryniak

Russia is a post-Communist country. Obvious enough, you might think, but the changes of recent years have seemed so dramatic and far-reaching that we have not always paused to reflect how much has failed to change, and to what extent Russian institutions and customs still bear the mark of the Communist past

Left: Moscow's Red Square: the old order changeth...but too slowly for some

GEOFFREY HOSKING

Surviving Communism

THE power structure of the Soviet Union is best understood as an interacting network of clans, sometimes internally bound by genuine kinship ties, but more often by shared political experience or loyalty to a common leader. Each authority figure, say the first secretary of a regional party committee, would gather round himself a coterie of clients and protégés, who would defend his interests, service his needs and generally advance his cause, while in return, if he was successful and climbed the ladder of promotion, he would raise them along with him, rather like a party of mountaineers. When Brezhnev became First Secretary of the Soviet Communist Party, he gathered round himself secretaries and advisers who had been associated with him earlier in his career, 'the Dnepropetrovsk mafia', as they were often called. All the way down the ladder the same practice was replicated at each level, and the ties of both obedience and loyalty thus generated constituted the sinews of the structure. This was the nomenklatura system, formalised and monitored in the file indexes (no doubt computerised in later years) in the Central Committee of the Soviet Communist Party.

The post-Soviet system has retained many of these features. Nearly all the political parties that have emerged since 1990 are centred around a small clique headed by a single leader. What divides them from one another is not ideology, but personal rivalry, and when they split and reform the reason is almost always personal conflicts. The president of Russia himself conforms to this stereotype: at all stages in his career Yeltsin, rather than create a political party — at which he has been very unsuccessful — has sought to surround himself with people he could trust. Immediately after the Soviet collapse, it was a circle of old regime non-conformists (if you like, liberals) from Sverdlovsk and Moscow. Nowadays, it is a medley of advisers from the 'power ministries', headed by his trusted personal bodyguard, Alexander Korzhakov.

The privatisation of trade and industry, though it is perhaps the most radical of the recent social transformations, has proceeded largely according to the same nomenklatura rules. Most of the newly privatised firms are either managed by ex-members of the nomenklatura elite, or are owned by consortia put together in the apparatus old boy network, usually using money stashed away in the final years of the old regime. This 'party gold' is such a sensitive subject that all attempts by the media to investigate it have met with a firm rebuff. In August 1991, immediately after the failed coup, Nikolai Kruchina, a senior CP official responsible for finances, died mysteriously after falling from his balcony. The KGB declared it a suicide, but the suspicion has remained that Kruchina was eliminated because he knew too much about the fate of the 'party gold'.

The other survivors from the old regime are its underground entrepreneurs, the activists of the 'black' or illegal economy. In the planned economy, enterprise directors had to do business with them in order to overcome the rigidities of the system: to obtain urgently needed spare parts, materials or fuel they offered bribes, backhanders or reciprocal 'services' in payment. Now that the black economy has been largely legalised, the personal relations struck up then have continued and flourished. Hence the hectic atmosphere of corruption and criminality which surrounds much Russian business.

Since the forces of law and order are also enmeshed in this system, each business needs its own protection, unless it can claim security through personal connections in the police. That is why most enterprise directors keep a personal bodyguard and hire armed guards to protect their premises. Sometimes clashes between them take place at the highest level: thus in December 1994, a squad from the entourage of Alexander Korzhakov, stormed a building belonging to the banking group Most, in order to demonstrate to its boss, Vladimir Gusinsky, that his protection — his 'roof' as it is often called — was not strong enough.

Some observers believe that some such interaction of criminal and official structures precipitated the Chechen war. It is curious, for example, that for three years after Dudayev's declaration of independence, there was little serious attempt to negotiate with him. Perhaps this is because highly-placed figures in Yeltsin's administration were actually doing nicely out of clandestine deals which involved the Chechen mafia, with its access to oil, drugs and other valuable assets. When these cosy arrangements broke down, Yeltsin's entourage advised him to go to war.

In the case of agriculture, the connection with the past is much more straightforward. Although it has been legal for some years now for collective farmers to lease plots of *kolkhoz* land for life, and to sell the produce they cultivate on the open market, very few have in fact done so, and even fewer have made a success of it. Collective farms have proved unwilling to release their members in this way, and even more reluctant to hand over good land to them. Those farmers who have set up on their own have found it difficult to raise credit to buy machinery, fertilisers and the other essentials of small-scale agribusiness.

The Duma has consistently refused to allow full-scale private ownership of land, and it is only recently that Yeltsin introduced it by decree. But leased land is less valuable as collateral for a loan, and so restricts the farmer's ability to raise credit. The result of all this is that the output of food remains miserably low. Most food shops are full of imported tins and packets; local food is scarce, expensive and poor quality.

The cliquish arrangements in politics and economics are cosy, personal and easy to understand. They resemble those of feudal Europe, when the salvation of the individual lay in attaching himself to a powerful baron. The problem is that in today's Russia the majority of the population is excluded from the mutual back-scratching (or feuding) and regards the 'barons' with cynicism and embitterment. Back in 1991-92 they were told that the new Russia would bring them freedom, property and a stake in a prosperous economy. It hasn't turned out like that at all for most of them.

If internal politics depends on which is the strongest clique, then Russians are inclined to treat international relations in a similar light. Security depends on attaching oneself to the most powerful alliance of barons. That is why most Russians believe that if NATO expands eastwards, that can only mean that the alliance belonging to the USA has demonstrated its superiority over that belonging to Russia. There are, of course, people, especially in the Foreign Ministry, who seek security on less primitive lines, through co-operation with international organisations, but their voices get drowned by the dominant perception of a zero-sum game.

Russia cannot decide whether it is now a nation-state which recognises the rights of other nation-states, or whether it is still an empire, the residual trustee of the Soviet Union, with an abiding right and duty to intervene in the affairs of its other former members. In some respects, it has behaved like a nation-state, for example in withdrawing its troops

Communist newspaper vendor sells New World *(Novyi Svet) St Petersburg 1996:
competing visions of the future*

peacefully from central Europe and the Baltic republics. But in other cases
it has tended to assert itself in the old imperial manner, by leaning heavily
on Moldavia, on Georgia (in Abkhazia) and on Tajikistan (in the name of
the common fight against 'Islamic fundamentalism'). It seems now to be
on the point of reincorporating Belarus, a step which many Russian
politicians hope will be the first stage towards restoring the Soviet Union.

Ironically the Communists, whose candidate Gennady Zyuganov may
be elected president in June, no longer represent the nomenklatura elite
— not the successful ones anyway, for they have all found comfortable
niches either in the private economy or in Yeltsin's power network.
Today's Communists represent the unsuccessful apparatchiks, plus the old,
the poor, the disadvantaged, army officers (many of them now poverty-
stricken and demoralised), and those dependent on the public budget.

It is almost true to say that the Communists have learnt nothing and forgotten nothing. But in fact they have learnt one thing: that at heart they are imperial Russian nationalists. That was true in Soviet days too, but was masked behind an internationalist rhetoric. Nowadays it is out in the open: they say they would restore the Soviet Union, and also revive the collectivist values of old Russia, with its heart in the *obshchina,* the village commune. Lenin must be spinning in the Mausoleum at the un-Marxist things his supporters now proclaim, but they have tapped the feelings of many Russians as they seldom did when they ruled the country.

One of the great gains of post-Soviet Russia has been the relative liberty of the media. Yeltsin's regime has not been blameless, but compared with any predecessor, its record on freedom of speech is estimable. But this is not just a result of greater state tolerance. Journalists, writers and editors have displayed great courage in widening freedom of expression and then defending the newly won frontiers. Lacking traditional means of censoring newspapers and television, those anxious to conceal compromising news have resorted to threatening, attacking and even murdering journalists, as a perusal of *Index*'s recent coverage demonstrates. The army, in particular, has done its best to keep them out of sensitive spots in Chechnya, and some journalists have displayed immense resourcefulness and courage to keep reliable information flowing.

If they come to power, the Communists cannot restore the old command economy. They would cause economic collapse and perhaps civil war if they tried. They would certainly face determined and highly placed opponents, able to summon up armed force. What they probably can do is renationalise some firms as part of a new corporate economy, protected from the harsh winds of global trade by tariffs and restrictions on the exchange of the rouble. If they do that, however, they will have to face the threat of mass starvation, since Russia depends on imports for so much of its food. At least there would be a return to queues and rationing.

There was never going to be any way of escaping from the Communist system painlessly. The unrewarded distress — shock without the therapy some call it — which most of the population has suffered during the transition was bound to restore some of the Communists' popularity. But no more than anyone else — less so, in fact — can the Communists now solve Russia's problems.

The great question now is not who wins the elections, which will really be a contest between successful Communists and unsuccessful Communists, but whether they take place at all in a tolerably credible

Mafia law and order

'The Mafia in this country always really existed, but the structures and the bureaucracy and the control of the Soviet empire — the USSR — has collapsed, there's been a need for the Mafia structures to take over. And it seems that way, it seems that while you're in a society where there are government controls but the government seems to be very lax, and there doesn't seem to be any real authority in the country. People are looking which way to go next; Mafia structures have introduced a sense of control, certainly at street level...'

'The Mafia exists at two very different levels. There's street Mafia, which is hoodlum Mafia, which is 300 gangs in Moscow maybe who occupy and carve up the turf. They own a stretch of street which they racketeer or they run a stretch of kiosks and these kiosks are obliged to buy from them and obliged to pay them protection money. And then there's Mafia which is really not so much Mafia but contacts, which is also illegal business, but it's illegal business based on connections, and who you know — maybe you have contacts in government, or in other organisations. And this isn't really a Mafia of "bang bang you're dead" kind of street fighting, this is a Mafia of semi-respectability. Everybody at one stage or another was making money in a illegal way, and huge amounts, the fortunes that were being made, the tens of millions of dollars stashed away in people's accounts in the West or wherever, this money was unlikely to have been made legally, but it's the tendency in this country for the people who made money this way to try and gain more respectability. And there's a whole drive towards respectability. You see this in banks, in businesses, in companies adopting western business practices and trying to clean their acts up.'

Excerpted from 'Bucks in the USSR', BBC Radio 4

form. If they do, then whoever wins, a big step will have been taken away from the post-Soviet politics of command and cliquishness, and towards a more open civic style, in which people believe they can vote for meaningful parties that have a hope of coming to power. In that sense, paradoxically, even a Communist victory might mean further progress away from Communism. ❑

Geoffrey Hosking *is professor of Russian history at the School of Slavonic and East European Studies, University of London*

BABEL

MEMBERS OF THE KGB RESERVE

Why we're not voting Communist

They served it well in their time, but the members of the old KGB know too much of the inner terror of the Party to give its new-style leaders a second chance

Lieutenant Colonel Yury Belousov: Zyuganov talks a lot. He's a politician. What he says is OK. It's sober; it seems fair. He's promising social guarantees. That's all fine. Who wants to be poor and lonely? But... there's a whole detachment there behind him. It's made up of people who used to drive around in Volgas, or Chaikas even. They were in power. They were there leading us into a glorious future in the darkest, most terrible way, through executions, prisons and camps. I've seen many people destroyed by the authorities for a careless word about being fed up with queues or something. I'm surprised so many have forgotten that these are the men who ordered the imprisonment of so many innocent people. And they now want to take power. If they win, they will never, ever relinquish power. Do you understand that?

Major Sergei Samoylov: I think that if Andropov had not succumbed to ill-health, the country would — in time — have been run by the secret police. People forget what kind of system we had then. Under Andropov in particular, the camps were getting fuller and fuller. We, 'the servants of the Party', had no doubt at all that a new wave of repressions had begun. As a result of stagnation the country had fallen behind the leading powers and there was a need for unpaid labour, there was a need for prisoners in labour camps because rumours were going around that the leaders of the KGB in collaboration with the Communist Party were preparing a new campaign of repressions throughout the Soviet Union.

Yu B: At the time, I had the impression that the leadership of the KGB thought the leaders of the Party were halfwitted. Leonid Brezhnev went to Helsinki and spoke at a congress there. The KGB sent a terse telegram to the regional administration ordering them to collect reactions from the population. And the bluff would begin. Officers would take newspapers and make their notes: '*Kolkhoz* worker Malyshnikov, agent known as Vasek, has established that the whole village of Ponteleyevka rejoices at the wise words of Leonid Ilich...' This really did happen. And all this gibberish got through to the very top, the Central Committee.

Lieutenant Colonel Valery Matveyev: Or take the reports of republican committees or the regional administration of the KGB. Every year they were dressed up as a single document and a note was sent to the Central Committee. It was the usual farce: 'enemy-influence is growing; the western special services are out in force; enemy propaganda is growing increasingly vicious, our young people are being corrupted...'

SS: But behind the bluff were all the broken lives. Unfortunately, cynicism was part and parcel of our job. But the things that went on in the Fifth Administration and the Third Central Board surprised even me, and I was in active service. KGB leaders made us launch 'the case of the spinal cripples'. This operation investigated people who had been invalids since childhood. One of these unfortunates (Vasilev I think his name was) had told foreign correspondents that in the Soviet Union invalids were treated worse than abroad. That was when it all started. Tapping, observation, terror and provocation — the whole hog. The persecution of these cripples was controlled by the Central Committee, where reports by the KGB top brass were regularly sent. Huge sums of money were spent, enough to supply wheelchairs for all the invalids in Moscow and provide special lifts in subways for them into the bargain.

Yu B: And the operations to trap young people! At one stage they decided to kill two birds with one stone: show the corrupting influence of the West on Soviet youth and demonstrate the threat of terrorism. It was a nightmare I'll never forget. They got to work on two young soldiers. It was a cheap strategy. The agent got to know the two conscripts and drank with them regularly. During one of these drinking sessions he started a conversation on how all those bastards from the Party Regional Committee should be shot, that sort of thing. The soldiers were drunk; they concurred. As a result they were accused of planning an act of terrorism against Party workers. One got 10 years in camp; the other 15. That was how the USSR fought its battle against terrorism.

SS: They used to go for students in the same sort of way, provoking them into saying things like the shops in America were stuffed with goods while here everything gets lost in black holes. They would get five to seven years in camp. Or take this. There was a rumour in Moscow that the tax on dogs was about to go up. A group of dog lovers decided to march through Red Square with their four-legged friends as a sign of protest. There was panic in the Lubyanka. They began to look for ways of compromising the dog owners to get a case together against them. High-level officials in the KGB seriously considered ways of bugging the dogs to monitor what their owners said. This is more than an anecdote: it's the history of the Communist Party of the Soviet Union.

Yu B: If they kept an eye on dog owners, they watched writers all the more. The houses where they lived and rooms in the Writers' Union were bristling with special apparatus. But even here things aren't that simple. Take Solzhenitsyn: he said that he was our enemy quite openly. Whatever they did to him in camp, however hard they tried to break him, he stood firm. Even the most abject prison guard respected him for his courage, though he might have hated him for his views.

Behind Zyuganov today, looms the shadow of Ivan Abramov, the head of the former Fifth Ideological Administration of the KGB. He was the one who organised the absurd trials we are talking about. It wasn't long ago that Irina Ratushinskaya was held in a camp in Mordovia. She was released in 1987, just a girl she was. She'd been given seven years' camp and five years' exile for one line of poetry: 'Russia breeds slaves and the poor.'

VM: If Anatoly Kryuchkov became the head of the Federal Security

Right: Gorky Park, Moscow: Lenin vandalized

Service tomorrow and A Dunayev head of the Interior Ministry, they and their sort would create martial Communism overnight. And there wouldn't be many who'd as much as squeal. After Moscow has been transformed into a camp, the provinces will be on their knees within a couple of days. I'm a professional; I know what I'm saying. The nightmare will start all over again. Once they are back in power they will never give it up. The heirs of the CPSU will never again permit themselves to make the same mistakes.

Yu B: The KGB did a lot to defend state interests. But the leadership turned its servicemen into slaves alongside everyone else. We were scared, same as everybody, perhaps more so because we saw for ourselves how people can be ground to dust. I'll never vote for Zyuganov. I know what the people behind him will do to this country once they get their hands on the levers of power. ❏

First published in Moskovskie novosti, *18-26 February 1996*

Translated by Irena Maryniak

JOHN LLOYD

A balance sheet

The charges against him are all too obvious, but the gains of Yeltsin's three years in office should not lightly be given up

THE Russian intelligentsia, dispirited, shorn of influence and broke, had a colloquium in the *Literaturnaya gazeta* in February on its relationship with power. Led off by the greatest of the surviving 60s bards, Bulat Okudzhava — who said that Yeltsin had turned away from a group which had been his staunchest supporters when he was elected five years ago, and now 'scorned' it because he and his cronies could not bear criticism — it was, in the main, a melancholy series of reflections. Most agreed with Okudzhava: lamented the loss of a leader who had held out a promise of renewal: those who remained reluctantly loyal — and none were robust about being so — fell back on a recognition that speech was now free and that the Communists would be worse. Their collective posture was well summed up by the writer Andrei Bitov: the mark of an intellectual, he said, was to stand for certain moral and intellectual values, and to *have nothing to do with power.*

Those members of the intelligentsia who had expected more and tried to assist Yeltsin achieve it have usually had their fingers burned: some have resigned, some were sacked, a few cling on for the usual reason that to leave would hand their place to someone worse. The most famous defector was the former prisoner of conscience Sergei Kovalev (*see page 54*), who served as Yeltsin's Human Rights Ombudsman, protested loudly and with great courage against the war in Chechnya (he spent many weeks under bombardment in Grozny, the Chechen capital) and finally resigned from the last of his official posts earlier this year. In his resignation letter of 24 January 1996, a little literary and polemical masterpiece, he laments that Yeltsin was unable to make the break from being a member of the Central Committee of the Communist Party of the Soviet Union to become...a human being.

It was a fine rhetorical flourish, but it was wrong. Yeltsin's record is, whatever else, that of an all-too-human being: or, as Solzhenitsyn said of him well, a man 'almost too Russian'. Kovalev's formulation puts him out of the reach of human moral choice: the problem for the Russian intelligentsia, and for all the Russians who will choose a president on 16 June, is that they must make precisely such a choice.

The charge sheet against Yeltsin is an easy one to fill. In five years, he has described a tragic arc from vibrant defender of democracy to a closeted, narrowed man, suspicious of previous allies, enclosed by a circle almost none of whom have any links with the democrats and liberals of the late 80s and early 90s.

Chechnya leads the charges. It is not clear why he did not move against the rebellious, criminalised state much more quickly after it declared de facto independence at the end of 1991: allegations that senior officials and generals profited from its arms and drug trading rings may have a purchase on the decision. But when, in late 1994, after the failure of semi-clandestine efforts by the federal counter-intelligence agency to overthrow the regime of General Dzhokar Dudayev in concert with the groups of Chechens opposed to him, he ordered a full-scale military invasion of the republic, it is clear that the decision was the worst of his career — whether as a Communist or an anti-Communist.

In the course of the attempt, he has demonstrated the weakness of Russian arms — a weakness which might have been expected, given the shocks to which the military have been subjected in the past decade, but which nonetheless was itself shocking to witness. A general staff openly riven and split on participation in the war, insubordinate officers at all levels, a soldiery sullen, desperate to avoid the draft and so poorly fed and provisioned that at times they could not mount simple missions. At times, it seemed as if their largest activity was selling their weapons to those with whom they were locked in combat.

Ironically, this very demonstration of weakness and incompetence in both the military and in the Interior Ministry troops may — surely must — stimulate a party of reform within the general staff to bring about structural changes in a force diminished but largely unreconstructed since Soviet times. Yet even if that happens, it has been a hideous price to pay — the more so since the undoubted threat to the Russian state and to many of its citizens in and out of Chechnya could have been addressed (but was not) by a variety of measures short of war.

That the refusal to face the Caucasian tangle before the violence unleashed in December 1994 should be plausibly ascribed to corruption at the highest levels is an indication of how far the rottenness in the state has gone. Corruption, endemic in Soviet times, is a rule of official and political life in post-Soviet times: and though it is impossible to imagine that the transition from command economy to some form of market could fail to be accompanied by a splurge of criminality, it is also true that the Yeltsin circle has set a bad example and never acted as a pole of relative probity. Instead, the president himself has granted very large tax and other concessions to make his friends rich, has spread state largesse about with a free hand and has tolerated a level of corruption around him which dwarfs anything else in the world. In the past two years in particular, Yeltsin has acquiesced in the grabbing of corporations worth billions of dollars — including Gasprom, the biggest enterprise in the world — by people who are simply unknown.

He has adopted great swathes of his nationalist — and now his Communist — opponents' programmes: now celebrating what would be an economically disastrous union with Belarus, then decreeing that the red flag — with a star, but shorn of the hammer and sickle — should again be recognised as a state banner of Russia. Once a campaigner against the power and omnipresence of the KGB, he has recreated many of the features of a security state: and his closest guide, protector and friend is General Korzhakov, the former KGB officer who followed him into (and back from) the wilderness in 1987, and who now constitutes a lowering, suspicious presence at every occasion. In the presidential campaign so far he has shown no compunction in mobilising television behind his campaign — silencing criticism, firing his one-time friend Oleg Poptsov from the chairmanship of Russian TV because of the latter's critical spirit (see page 64).

For many, it has become wholly clear that Boris Yeltsin never wished to achieve power in order to build democracy, but merely wished to destroy the Soviet system to achieve power. It seems clear enough that the only possible reason to vote for him is, indeed, that Gennady Zyuganov, leader of the Communist Party, is likely to be worse — though even that is debated.

Yet a case can be made for Yeltsin in more positive terms. For he can still be seen as a man who has the remnants of a vision of a freer Russia in

Anti-Yeltsin demonstration Moscow 1996: on the wrong side of the balance sheet

him, and who would still define his life's work as seeking to achieve it. It is a case which has worn threadbare, and it is impossible to tell if it will stand up to the exigencies of a second term, were he to win one in June. But it should be made.

The country has the institutions of a state governed by law. The constitution (of December 1993) may have been adopted through large-scale falsification: written in the aftermath of the shelling of the Russian Parliament, it is heavily pro-presidential, giving Russia's fledgling parties little formal scope for development. The constitutional court was unconstitutionally abolished by the president in the aftermath of the October 1993 events, and was slow to be recreated (though it now is): it has so far not played a very active role in adjudicating abuses.

But the institutions are there, and they have tended to strengthen themselves. The Duma (lower house) and Federation Council (upper house) have reflected the new majorities produced by the December 1995 elections: they have the power of influence, of legislative initiative and of denial of agreement to the budget and other legislation: and though the presidential administration is swollen and powerful, it has not mounted a challenge. The two and a half years since the shelling of the White House has not been a time of steadily tightening authoritarianism, as many thought it would be at the time: instead, it has been a time of contradictions, of retreats here and advances there.

Advances, most of all, in the economy — though few which have benefited the mass of people. After nearly four years of plans which part worked then wholly failed, a series of policies were adopted at the beginning of 1995, backed by the International Monetary Fund, which have seen inflation brought down to 25-30 per cent annually (it was at that level each month two years ago); the budget deficit lowered to six per cent and the rouble strengthening against the hard currencies. Russia has instituted a unique form of 'slow shock therapy' — the result of unremitting struggle between liberal and conservative politicians and economists, which the liberals seem slowly to be winning.

The slowness has been bad for the people, who have had to endure the effects of the transition much longer than those in other former Communist states. The fall in living standards for the majority, the fall in production and the constant interruptions to services have produced an insecure and harried population, whose male death rate — an astonishing average of 57 years — reflects the arduousness of the times. So distorted was its economy, so much in thrall to military production, so overstaffed and uncompetitive, Russia — like other post-Soviet states — could not escape a hard landing. The only saving grace was to make the shock sharp — a strategy Yeltsin backed, but then backed away from when political support for it collapsed. But he has appeared to realise he cannot return to command economics — and thus Russia has lurched towards a 'normal' economy, though without any certainty of succeeding in it.

He has rarely been an inspirational leader, except at the beginning of his run for power: more frequently in recent years, he has been a disgraceful one, appearing drunk on several public occasions (or, in the case of his 'visit' to Ireland in 1994, not appearing). He has claimed parity with the main western states for a country manifestly not at their economic level. He has been dismissive of, or threatening to, many of the leaders of the former Soviet states around Russia.

But he has confined his 'imperialism' to vague threats and growlings. The 'union' between Belarus and Russia is a mess, but it is a mess produced most of all by Alexander Lukashenka, the genuinely authoritarian president of Belarus: Yeltsin grasped at a treaty of union because it was an election ploy, not because Russia had forced Belarus back into an empire. Ukraine shows every sign of wishing to remain a separate state; and though Yeltsin has snubbed the Ukrainian leaders, he has not threatened the state's independence. The record of Russia towards these states has not been uniformly bad: where Georgia was reduced to acquiescence with the assistance of Russian arms, the Baltics have been left alone.

Why talk only of Yeltsin and Zyuganov? Because, two months before the vote, it seems as if they will be the two contestants in the final round. As this is written, a 'third force' is trying to coalesce around General Alexander Lebed: and Grigory Yavlinsky and Vladimir Zhirinovsky are also candidates — as is Mikhail Gorbachev. None, it seems, presently, will be able to match the leads which Zyuganov and Yeltsin are building up.

For the democrats, the failure to produce a strong candidate around whom they could unite is particularly bitter. Yavlinsky has the best claims on that: he has, in four years of opposition, continued to represent a centrist-liberal position. He has been strongly against the Chechen war: supported freedoms: supported a liberal economy. But jealousies among the democrats have been at least as strong as those among the nationalists (and much stronger than among the Communists and their allies, where habits of discipline appear to have lingered). Yavlinsky, too, has been abrasive and apparently uninterested in agreements: the result has been that Yeltsin, against the odds, has retained the reluctant support of a large number of those whose consciences he has outraged.

This is not a pre-election scene to bring joy to any hearts, Russian or foreign. But it may not produce despair. ❏

John Lloyd is former Moscow correspondent of the Financial Times *(1991-1995). He is now writing a book on the first five years of the new Russian state*

SERGEI KOVALEV

Old griefs revisited

In Russia today, human rights is a political and legal issue. The future of democracy depends on their being given priority

HUMAN RIGHTS violations remain the most painful problem in Russia today. Human rights are protected by the constitution; their observation is guaranteed by international agreements to which Russia is a signatory; and everywhere they are abused — overtly and crudely.

All Russian politicians talk 'human rights', its slogans feature in the pre-election posters of many political parties, but no-one is prepared to defend them and when a choice arises between political interests and legal principles, political interests invariably prevail. Legal arguments are used by the authorities and the opposition as a political lever, but neither the law nor human rights present a serious obstacle to political expediency. They remain pure rhetoric, often shrouding blatantly arbitrary rule.

Sending its troops into Chechnya, the present administration spoke of the need to restore constitutional order in the region and protect the constitutional rights of its citizens. Since then, we have seen tens of thousands killed, hundreds of thousands of refugees, torture, summary execution, looting, disinformation or lies from the military and civil authorities, restricted freedom of movement, attacks on press freedom, the collapse of the rule of law, the falsification of electoral results, ethnic discrimination...the sorry list could go on. Chechnya has become not only the ground for large-scale arms dealing and colossal extortion, but the testing zone for a new totalitarianism.

And a pretty successful one at that. Social apathy and xenophobia are rife. Disappointment with democracy and humanitarianism has diverted public attention towards new priorities. 'State', Communism, fascism are more than abstractions in Russia today. They are supported by powerful political groups, with set programmes and organisational structures, electoral constituencies and a readiness to fight for power. We witnessed their success in the December 1995 parliamentary elections. The run-up to the presidential elections in June 1996 has so far confirmed that the battle for power, for the hearts and minds of Russia's citizens, is not being fought between democratic forces on the one hand and totalitarian forces on the other, but between varying forms of the new totalitarianism.

The struggle is taking place in an arena where there is no room for authentic democratic values. What our state institutions, Communists and nationalists call 'human rights' bears no relation to the rights of the individual. It merely indicates the political, economic and social interests of select groups or individuals. In official parlance, the protection of these interests is the defence of the 'collective rights' of different segments of the population.

For our ruling party, the interests of the state represent the highest value. In fact these are no more than the interests of the ruling 'corporation': the caste of high-level civil and military officials in the ruling apparatus, central and regional. The development of the grouping was screened by democratic rhetoric. Its original function was to redistribute state property and re-establish spheres of economic and political influence; to squeeze out the old Communist nomenklatura from key posts. Having achieved its principal aim, the corporation is seeking to keep its spoils. The rule of law is not always to its advantage. Its aims are better served by the time-honoured principle of *'derzhavnost'*: the principle of the state, over and above the individual and society. The concomitant dangers are already apparent. Political reforms have been reversed; authoritarian rule is preferred; policy-making is unpredictable and covert; a nationalist ideology has been formulated. Increasingly, individual rights will be subsumed to 'the interests of the people', for which read the interests of the authorities.

On the opposing side stand forces unified by Communist rhetoric. On the basis of evident economic and social miscalculations, this grouping is attracting a significant contingent of electors nostalgic for times when there was no need to answer for anything, when the authorities guaranteed a life that was impoverished but relatively free of anxiety. Democratic-sounding slogans notwithstanding, a Communist victory is bound to prompt a wave of revanchism, aggressive isolationism, and the destruction of those weak shoots of democracy that have appeared in Russia over the past decade. State Communism will be even more

Grozny January 1996: demonstration in favour of Shamil Basayev, hero of Budennovsk

disastrous for human rights than the policy of the present authorities: for the debasement of individuality is intrinsic to the Communist programme.

The third organised force in Russian politics is nationalism. This plays a supportive role: on the one hand it tacitly feeds state and Communism with a complimentary dose of fascism and xenophobia; on the other, it provides an outlet for social anxiety. It is a context in which human rights simply do not apply. Strangely enough, the best example of the way in which ethnic supremacy transforms human rights can be seen in the way the authorities of national republics within the Russian Federation often pay scant attention to civil and political rights while fiercely defending their national or state rights. In regions such as Tatarstan, Bashkiria, Tuva or Chechnya, the level of human rights abuses is notably higher than in Russia as a whole. Clearly, the 'nationalisation' of Russian policy will make no difference to regional abuse, but rather increase its level in the country as a whole.

Any one of these political forces could triumph in Russia; their victory will mean defeat for political reform, and the negation of the priority (or at least the parity) of human rights over the principle of political expediency. The tough talking will begin soon enough, not just with Russian citizens, but with the West — doubtless provoking an equally tough response. Yet the notion of human rights in Russian democratic circles is not so very different from the western one. Depressingly, though, many democrats see human rights not as the foundation of democracy, but as something secondary, emerging from economic or political reform — which is one reason for Russia's failure to achieve democratic change.

Much could be said, and fairly, about the fact that the Russian tradition and mentality is not the most fertile ground for human rights. But any efforts by democrats to surmount this tradition, and change the mentality of their fellow citizens, have been outrageously paltry. The defence of human rights has informed neither affairs of state nor education. And this explains not just the political decline of the democrats, but their fragmentation. While debating the details of economic programmes or foreign and home policy, they have ignored the common humanitarian values they all share.

If civil rights organisations still function in Russia today, if a free press exists, it is thanks not to Yeltsin, but to democratically oriented politicians, social and human rights activists and ordinary, decent people.

Should Yeltsin win the June elections, the most important task facing democratic organisations will be to instil in the public mind an awareness of human rights as the foundation for state and society. The second, no less vital task will be the creation of a network of human rights organisations capable of defending citizens' rights and supporting democratic civil associations. To establish a broad spectrum of human rights work is the only way of creating a social basis for democratic political parties, assisting their consolidation and ultimately increasing their electoral success. In present circumstances, this sort of work has a distinct political significance. It is directed towards the establishment of an alternative political model for the country, opposed to the policy of the present authorities and, even more, to the Communist and nationalist models.

We have come to view work in the field of human rights and education in non-political terms. But in Russia today human rights is a legal and political issue. Any more moral or honest polity will depend on the priority given to them.

This kind of work is exceptionally difficult in any circumstances; under the Communists it may be dangerous. And it is here that the experience gained by dissidents in the 1960s, 70s and 80s may once again prove useful. Their struggle against Communism had a vital moral influence during the early stages of Russia's reforms, as the old system collapsed. Later, in the construction of a new state system, it was harder to make use of the negative experience of dissent, and the involvement of former rights activists in public life was severely circumscribed. Most chose not to return from emigration; of the dozens living in Russia, just a few went into politics. But I am sure that, if the threat of a totalitarian revival arises, whatever its rhetoric, many former dissidents will re-emerge.

That, I believe, is where my own future lies. I do not know whether we will have the strength or wherewithal to stir public opinion into resistance. But fight we must. Or we will not be worthy of our freedom. ❏

Sergei Kovalev was the head of the Presidential Commission on Human Rights until his resignation on 23 January 1996. He is currently setting up a human rights institution which will seek to consolidate all human and civil rights organisations in the Russian Federation

Translated by Irena Maryniak

ALEKSEI SIMONOV

Censorship yesterday, today, tomorrow

Russian journalism is at a crossroads. Since Communism and a free press cannot coexist, argues a veteran Russian journalist, the first task of a free press is to prevent a Communist victory in the June elections

'Without seeing the need for unlimited press freedom, one can perceive nothing.'
Fyodor Dostoevsky

I HAVE in my personal archive the first edition of Mikhail Bulgakov's novel *The Master and Margarita*, published in two issues of the journal *Moskva* (1966/67). The journals are scarcely a rarity; they are owned by many lovers of literature of my own generation and the next, and it would not be worth keeping them in an archive if it were not for one thing: the text in my journals contains notes and inserts of all the passages extracted by the censor when the work was first published — from individual words and lines to paragraphs running into dozens of pages. An official's scissors shredded the body of one of the greatest novels of the twentieth century and my copy is a unique monument to Soviet culture — insolent, senseless, fearful not only of free expression, but of itself. Two years later, the novel was published in full, and one might consider the whole episode a silly mistake if the archives of so many other people did not contain similarly censored books, articles and films, if we did not remember the songs, plays, novels and television programmes which we were prevented from seeing for years or which we saw disfigured and dishonoured. Soviet censorship, invoked to guard the great Communist lie, had been so long embroiled in that lie that any unusual word, any original thought seemed to it to hint at truth, awakening fear and a desire to escape with scissors and interdictions.

At the same time, the constant necessity to slip between the Scylla and Charybdis of censorship, instilled in writers, historians and cinematographers a special subtlety of style; it taught them the art of allusion, metaphor, richness of intonation. At times literature slipped through. For journalism it was harder, because even a straightforward, non-judgemental presentation of facts became impossible if it did not cohere into an ode to the all-conquering Communist ideal. Fear prompted self-censorship even among the best. But it also reminded us all of the thin line between truth and 'truth'.

We lived by double standards. We distinguished between two truths: one for a narrow circle of friends and another, the official truth, appropriate for meetings, newspaper articles and TV interviews. And the fear of confusing these two accompanied us everywhere. But the fear was also a kind of watershed between truth and falsehood. Now it has gone, or nearly gone, and if it remains at all among young journalists, it can only be genetic. The only remaining division between truth and falsehood lies in a weak perception of morality, a perception unattainable to so much post-Soviet journalism. But the abolition of state censorship has not helped journalists to develop a real aversion to censorship itself, and in recent years it has begun to appear again, often in unrecognised forms but no less influential for all that. It is underpinned by the administrative and economic measures now in place; it is reflected in the pressures which can be brought to bear by criminal organisations; and is inherent in the continuing tradition of self-censorship.

Administrative censorship, for example, is widespread in the provinces. What can the authorities of a town, region or *oblast* do if they are displeased with what the local paper is writing about them? There are a number of alternatives. They can induce all official bodies — from the fire brigade to the tax inspector — suddenly to show an interest in the publication. Even if it proves impossible to achieve any improvement in its attitude, the newspaper or TV company will be held in check for six months by constant inspections, audits and the like. Or they can seize the account of the publication in connection with an inspection of its bank; or cancel its registration and under that pretext confiscate its editorial

St Petersburg 1996: 50 years a hero; could he make a comeback?

offices. There is the possibility of harsher pressure: the authorities can summon the head of the registering body and on the following day there will appear another newspaper with the same name, logo and, naturally, a new editor or editorial team. This is no fantasy. The newspapers *Lyuberetskaya pravda* and *Sovetskaya Kalmykia* which had this kind of trick played on them have been trying for two years to protest through the courts. This is irrespective of decisions taken by the presidential judicial chamber which examined the dispute twice and came out in support of the wronged newspapers.

There is another method which entails taking a newspaper to court for any one article and accusing it either of libel or of offending the honour and dignity of officials in the administration. This is not confined to the provinces. According to the editor of the popular Moscow paper *Izvestiya*, he continuously fights up to 23 cases of this sort at a time. This is possible because, by law, the prosecution bears no responsibility — either moral or financial — for its suit.

As regards economic measures, the state monopoly on the distribution of newspapers and radio frequencies remains. With the system of subsidies in operation until 1995, there was always the possibility of refusal. Today, subsidies are given only to state-owned media, and are pretty unequivocally reflected in their political stance. A law on advertising passed recently has proved a useful lever for press manipulation. Verdicts on the 'honesty' of advertising are decided, frequently, by bribes, and officials use the threat of fines as a means of pressurising the media.

If it is to survive, no mass medium in Russia today can allow itself full 'transparency' in its financial policy. Everyone is forced to 'sell himself' to some degree, to find unofficial forms of financial support. This makes the mass media vulnerable to shadowy organisations and hidden forms of blackmail.

In the past two years alone over 10 journalists have been killed either to prevent publication of material they had collected or in revenge for what they had already published. The murders of Dmitry Kholodov and Vladislav Listyev are merely the most widely publicised of these. In addition, of course, there are forms of pressure such as threats to journalists, their families and children. They come not only from criminal groupings but also from corrupt agencies associated with the Interior Ministry. Regional administrations and local militias are frequently connected with suspect organisations and their treatment of journalists (especially those who write on corruption and irregular behaviour by the militia) is essentially nothing short of criminal. The Glasnost Defence Foundation (GDF) has documented cases in many places including Vladivostok, Mordovia, Volgograd, Vologda and Voronezh.

At the end of 1994, the GDF carried out a survey, published as *Journalists and journalism in the Russian provinces*. To the question 'Have you experienced pressure from the authorities?', 25 per cent of the 1,200 journalists questioned answered 'yes'; while another 27 per cent said that they had been the object of pressure or threats from political, commercial or criminal groups. One can scarcely suppose that, in conditions where every second journalist is subjected to pressure or threats, self-censorship can fully disappear.

R USSIAN journalism is at a crossroads. Having ceased to be the 'executor of the will of the Party', it has quickly taken upon itself the role of the 'fourth estate', without considering that the fourth estate is actually not the press but public opinion, in whose name and on whose behalf the media operate.

I cannot share the conviction of many foreign observers that the restoration of Communism as an all-defining state ideology is out of the question because Russia has a free press which will not permit this to happen. Just as democracy itself remains fragile throughout the former USSR — with the possible exception of the Baltic States — so the press has not yet found its place in Russian democracy. Having lost a great deal, journalism has not yet found a steady sense of its own dignity.

The economic state of the media, best depicted as a battle for survival, does not allow for the development of a journalistic community with shared ethical standards, an impatience with those who fail to live up to these standards and solidarity in the face of external pressure. For this reason, the restoration of old-style Communism is, in my view, entirely possible.

Press statements from the ideologues of 'the new, social democratically-oriented' Communist Party indicate that changes in the law on the mass media are viewed as a priority after a 'quick victory'. History demonstrates that Communists and a free press cannot coexist.

But the issue does not lie solely with the Communists. The press, shaky in its new democratic mode, is in no position to resist determined state pressure. This was demonstrated by our 'democratic' authorities in January, in Kizlyar and Pervomayskoye. Not a single journalist was permitted into the area where the action was taking place; the world, including President Yeltsin, was fed with lies by representatives of the power structures and the security services. In the course of a year's war in Chechnya the GDF has identified about 350 instances of abuses of journalists' rights and crimes against the press. About as many are documented on the territory of the former USSR (excluding the Baltic States) without any war at all.

The first task of a free, or even 'conditionally free', press remains the prevention of the victory of a Communist candidate in the presidential elections. I realise how curious this must sound to the European ear, attuned to the tradition of a restrained, objective mass media. But such is the real Russia today. We shall not survive a Communist renaissance. To prevent it, the press must be more balanced and restrained, more professional and less partisan. Failing this, we shall become the victims of a paradox formulated so excellently by Igor Malashenko, director general of NTV, the best of Russia's independent TV stations: 'It is widely held that the elections will be won by whoever controls television. This is self-evidently absurd. Anyone with eyes and ears will have seen twice over that in Russia, whoever controls television, loses elections.' The experience of two election campaigns confirms that Malashenko is right. Furthermore this is true not only of television but of the press as a whole. The Communists can be defeated only by intelligence, not by media pressure. Will the press as it now is be capable of achieving this? With the presidential election planned for June, we are likely to find out soon. ❏

Aleksei Simonov *is head of the Glasnost Defence Foundation*

Translated by Irena Maryniak

OLEG POPTSOV

Capital television

The entry of private capital into Russian broadcasting bodes no good says its former chief, dismissed by President Yeltsin in February this year

It has been suggested that you were removed as chairman of All-Russian State Television and Radio because of your book, Chronicles of Tsar Boris. *Others have said that it was prompted by your handling of television. Which version of the story do you prefer?*

Oleg Poptsov

IHAVE a third version of my own: that there are financial groupings
seeking to take control of television. I don't think that the book
influenced the president's decision, though it undoubtedly had an effect on
the people who keep him informed. I was introduced to Boris Berezovsky
about two years ago now. Boris Adamovich outlined his ideas in the style
characteristic to him: we've come to grips with this, we've been here;
we're moving in there. It took two hours. Then he talked for an hour and
a half about selling shares in the channel. He made his proposal. I listened
to it all and said I couldn't agree with his political analysis. Russia, with its
traditions and mentality, should have strong state television. In a country
such as this, television is an instrument of government.

Subsequently, of course, Berezovsky found his partner in Alexander
Yakovlev, former head of Channel 1. Today Boris Berezovsky controls
Russian Public Television (ORT) and has nearly 30 per cent of Channel
6. The fact that Berezovsky was actively engaged in securing my removal
is clear enough. That was always the case, and I don't think it was ever a
secret.

People say that the final decision was made not by the president but by
someone in his circle. These conversations make me smile. They are
absurd. I used to hear them as a child. Then again as a young man. 'Stalin
knew nothing'; 'Stalin was deceived.' The president makes his own
decisions. In my case he did it with particular emphasis. Furthermore, he
deliberately announced it in Yekaterinburg — during his electoral
campaign. He was afraid that if he did so in Moscow he would meet an
avalanche of protest.

*When the events in Pervomayskoye and Novogroznensky were taking place neither
ORT, nor Russian State Television, nor the independent channel NTV, nor Radio
Mayak, nor Radio Rossii gave any idea what was happening. All we heard were
official lies. So I set to, twiddling the knob on my radio, just as I used to do in the
old days, to pick up 'voices' from abroad. And from them I discovered how things
really stood. A week later, all the information I had heard on foreign radio was
confirmed by our newspapers. They are not subjected to censorship as heavily as the
electronic media. Seeing this victorious offensive by censorship, did you not feel
vindicated after your dismissal? After all, if you can't withstand the stifling of free
speech, isn't it better to go?*

W E seem to disagree in our assessment of what and how Russian TV reports. There is no hidden censorship; only access to information or lack of it.

Russian TV and radio are only concerned with the official version, then I would fail to understand why I had been dismissed. But I was reprimanded for the 'negative programming' which in fact was simply a reflection of the reality in which we live. We were broadcasting information about the life we lead more fully than any other of the electronic media. We took full advantage of our greatest achievement: free speech.

We have always tried to offer our viewers and listeners a maximum of what we know; and to explore, as much as we can, what we don't know. I sent a team to report on Pervomayskoye. We set up a dish opposite the village (everyone photographed it). As you know, access to the village was denied while military action was taking place. But we still got in; we reported on what was happening, on whether trenches had been dug and weapons stored in advance. It provoked a very sharp reaction from the power ministries.

I rang the Federal Security Service headquarters myself. I failed to reach Mikhail Barsukov — they said he was in Dagestan — and I spoke to his deputy. 'What are you doing?' I said. 'It's crazy to block information! It's bound to hit back at you tomorrow. Let people through! They'll get in anyway, illegally. We seem to be playing silly buggers all over again. What on earth for?' The deputy agreed, but nothing changed.

I can't agree that we released truncated, censored information. But I shan't try to persuade you not to listen to the BBC. ❑

Excerpts from a press conference following the dismissal of Oleg Poptsov on 15 February 1996, published in Literaturnaya gazeta *6 March 1996*

Translated by Irena Maryniak

DANILA GALPEROVICH

Party political messages and the direct method

Presidential candidates discover the power of public relations. Pressing the flesh and chatting up the journalists give the Communist leader a head start

THE RESPONSE of Russian electors to western-style party political broadcasts became transparently clear in the result of the December 1995 elections to the State Duma. Neither the image of that happy family, off to vote for the ruling block 'Our Home is Russia'; nor those macho generals Alexander Lebed and Boris Gromov, in full military attire, calling for votes for The Congress of Russian Communities and My Fatherland; nor even that plump maiden dreaming of a fling with Vladimir Zhirinovsky in the ad for the Liberal Democrats attracted more than passing attention among viewers. And the Communist Party, which received over 150 seats in the Duma, achieved its result despite rather than because of its TV advertising which showed its leaders calling for votes against a backcloth of scarlet banners.

In 1993, Russia's Choice presented the Russian public with a well-nourished looking dog wistfully awaiting the return of its master from the polls. Many people, especially the old — for whom economic reform had brought nothing but poverty and loss of security — took the ad as an insult. Vladimir Zhirinovsky, on the other hand, spent his airtime delivering personal statements heaped with promises. They assured the Liberal Democratic Party's election victory. Zhirinovsky had found a new way of reaching the hearts and minds of the populace. 'I am the man to

Duma elections, Moscow 1995: Russians' choice

set this country to rights. And fast,' he seemed to say. It was all much like soap; viewers approved and voted accordingly.

In 1995, however, the Communists didn't make use of Zhirinovsky's recipe. They relegated television to second place, and went for direct contact with electors in the provinces instead. Their leader, Gennady Zyuganov, travelled the country, talking to his supporters. His meetings with local administrations were reported in newspapers and on television: this was real advertising. Zyuganov did no more than appropriate the techniques of his opponents, Mikhail Gorbachev and Boris Yeltsin, who gained most support and popularity when they left their limousines and went walkabout. He also worked hard on his image as an even-handed politician: respect for the Orthodox Church, tolerance of private property, no calls for revolution. And his meetings with electors were well prepared

— less political meetings than academic seminars.

The public relations organisation responsible for this new style was the 'Spiritual Heritage Foundation'. In exchange, its leading figures were assured of places in the Communist faction in the Duma and became parliamentary deputies. They prepared Zyuganov's pre-election speeches and worked out a strategy which ensured that, in the regions, the Communist Party was represented by people known throughout the country (the former chairman of the Supreme Soviet of the USSR, Anatoly Lukyanov, for example, or Emergency Committee member, Valentin Varennikov).

The Foundation is also in charge of the Party's pre-election strategy for the presidential elections in June. Communists should no longer rely solely on the support of low-waged workers and pensioners, Zyuganov said in January. They should work more with the professional classes: teachers, health workers, military and industrial scientists (all underpaid and known to be discontented).

Tactics towards the press have also changed. If in the past Communists were wary of interviews for fear of misrepresentation, they are now completely open to the media. In early March, parliamentary correspondents were not a little surprised when the entire leadership of the Communist Party took to shaking hands with them, and chatting at every chance encounter in the corridor. As it emerged later, a meeting of the Communist Party faction in the Duma had decided that journalists should now be shown maximum respect. It was a strong move given the increasingly negative stance of the authorities to the media.

Today, comments from the presidential administration on any political events are increasingly hard to come by. Employees of the presidential administration are permitted to invite foreigners into their offices in Moscow's Old Square only with the personal permission of the head of the administration or his deputy. As the presidential elections draw near, the Kremlin will doubtless become more open to journalists. But if Boris Yeltsin fails to reach electors and journalists directly, rather than through prepared statements and broadcasts, his victory over Zyuganov, his main rival, may well be in doubt. ❑

Danila Galperovich *is a journalist with the Postfactum news agency, Moscow*

Translated by Irena Maryniak

ALINA VITUKHNOVSKAYA

BEN ARTS/CAMERA PRESS

The crest of a rave

The generation who first experienced freedom have become the tools of a new totalitarianism, as chilling and pervasive as its predecessors

IN 1994, the young people of Moscow believed they were free. It seemed that their generation was the first in Russia with the right to experience freedom — an apolitical, non-ideological freedom for which they had not needed to struggle. It was there gratis, like manna from heaven.

My own sense of the artificial, surrogate nature of this 'freedom', its hidden agenda, was based only on intuition, a sense of the temporal, stillborn and extraneous quality of youth culture then. It had no connection with politics. Like many others of my age, I was convinced that our world and the world of politics were parallel universes. We felt certain we were outside the system. The trends followed by young people — new music, raves, synthetic drugs, psychedelic art — were not dangerous in themselves. Or at least they should not have become a more serious problem for us than for western countries.

'So who are the users of LSD on this side of the western border?' I wrote in the journal *Novoye vremya* in 1994. 'The establishment, the nouveaux-riches, students, creative professionals who want to galvanise the "cadaver of art" by fixing it with psychedelic solution. The circle of people using LSD will remain closed even if it grows every year. Russian society will swallow yet another dish of the age, stewed in a juice of its own making.'

These words were, I believe, the reason for my arrest by the security services (*Index* 1/1996). They hoped I would give them information about people connected with the drugs trade: above all, the children of influential figures, to compromise them and their parents, to manipulate and blackmail them for political ends.

The lines I wrote two years ago seem naive to me now. They reflect only the psychological essence of the phenomenon, which has little import in the picture as a whole. It is a picture in which there are no longer any personal psychological or moral problems. Here there is no space even for individual personality, only for violence against the personality through its manipulation. It is a picture which reveals the shadowy outlines of a shrouded dictatorship.

In prison, these outlines became glaringly apparent to me. 'It can't be true! Not in Moscow, in 1994!' I wrote there, desperate and unable to believe. But that is how it was. And how it is. And Big Brother looks on with a caustic grin at one and all: those who cry out in vain against injustice and arbitrary rule, and those who — wittingly or not — conform to the system.

What has happened to the young over the past two years? What of the people I wrote about then? The movement which I thought would be brief and stillborn remains: static, petrified, with the same unconsidered, mechanical drive.

When I was released from prison, instead of feeling dislocated and out of touch as I feared, I found that time had lagged behind. People who regarded themselves as progressives seemed to have run aground in their own complacency. The rave movement (which likes to call itself the rave 'culture') evokes the image of a crazed old man, rummaging in a dustbin. It is a senility born of the refusal to recognise that one stage in life has culminated in consummate ideological and aesthetic failure. They cry, even now, that they are living for the future. If so, the future is time in stasis.

They have created a cult of monotonous sound, of unremarkable — if uninhibited — dance in clubs where faces are indiscernible in the dark and individuality is devoured by an anonymous organism convulsed in primordial movement. And they have become indistinguishable. They have made a cult of drugs deprived of their 'mystical essence', a cheap, poisonous fix for a generation afraid to look at itself, which claims that it has overstepped the limits of its — actually shrunken — consciousness.

I remain convinced that the factors making the drugs scene so much worse [today] are political... Drugs have become a means of control, a form of government

They have been dubbed the 'rave and blotter' generation because they have not shown themselves capable of anything else. And they respond to the tag like pets to a master tempting them with tinned feed.

Their morality had never been bound by the hypocrisy of the system. It was never dictated by law, nor fettered to convention. It was conditioned by nothing but morality itself. I have never dared judge or suspect their integrity. I thought they could be malicious, aggressive, destructive; I allowed them every quality except degeneracy. I would have forgiven them any evil (evil can be great, evil can be art). But craven is nothing other than craven: insignificant, impoverished and calculating.

It was not generic to them. But when the system they had rejected and ignored extended its tentacles into their madness they suddenly came to move to the rhythm of dictatorship — without turning off the music, without breaking off the dance, with no change of expression on their faces. With no surprise or resistance, as though this was how it had always been. The hidden hand became apparent soon enough. Everyone knew who controlled the clubs and pushed the drugs. They were being watched. And they watched one another.

They were blackmailed with what they had once thought to be their freedom. Their freedom became a crime. And falling in line with the aims

A generation which takes freedom for granted has no inkling how to defend it. The generation for whom freedom is akin to nature, something outside the reaches of human will, has accepted its loss as something which cannot be resisted.

And even those who understood the causes of their loss of freedom, did not seek ways of resistance or want to rebel. The system selected its slaves faultlessly and anticipated the lack of resistance, allowing the 'rave and blotter' generation its toys. They were permitted not to change their lifestyle, their music, their language. They were allowed to sell drugs under the control of the security services. The more trustworthy ones control those who are less so. When the security services need to report on work that they have done, the trustworthy betray the less trustworthy or superfluous figures, those who have been accessories to the drugs trade, or those who have had nothing to do with it. It makes no difference.

The drugs myth is well and truly over. It has been replaced by a harshly organised business, 'legalised' for those who pay a given percentage of their profits, and dangerous for those who are potential victims of the security men who mind the accounts.

The effects of drugs, popular among the young in Moscow today, have nothing in common with those of the synthetic substitutes available in 1994. There were practically no real addicts among the kids I interviewed then. They were adventurers, 'travellers' between the worlds. The absence of any real danger in taking these drugs, their unobtrusive accessibility, created a sense of distance between the individual and the side effects which could arise in the long run. Now that drug taking is allied to high risk, to avoid making the transaction more often than necessary, the user will buy so much at once that he is likely to lose all sense of proportion. The dose taken often proves fatal.

Clean and cheap synthetic psychedelic drugs and harmless pharmaceutical stimulants have disappeared. Alternatives of indefinite quality are here instead, cut with washing powder, or some other poisonous substance, and costing a fortune. I know of cases of serious — even lethal — poisoning connected with their use. The season of deaths has begun. One after another people are dying, having swapped the amphetamines now unavailable in Moscow, for opium or heroin.

The number of full-blown addicts has risen dramatically. And those who have become addicts are often people whose creative abilities are unique. The rave generation has destroyed its own geniuses. Perhaps it was the system which removed them: for genius protests, genius is destructive and dangerous to the authorities.

Comparing the situation two years ago with the way things stand today, I remain convinced that the factors making the drugs scene so much worse are political. With the security services in charge of the 'battle' against drugs; with rising numbers of small dealers or occasional users destroying themselves in prison (where the psychological and physical harm done to inmates often exceeds that inflicted by drugs); with the number of informers higher than the number of potential victims — the quality of drugs is lower than ever. While their price is constantly growing, increasing numbers of people are succumbing to addiction. For good. Drugs have become a means of control, a form of government.

A youth, caught with a drug which he is perhaps trying out for the first time or which was specially slipped him by 'well-wishers', is worked over physically and morally, often in contravention of all norms of judicial procedure. They transform him into a poisoned animal; they describe to him the perspectives of life in prison and then, as an act of mercy, offer him an alternative: co-operation. It can happen to anybody.

The system knew well that it was right in its choice to turn the 'rave and blotter' generation into a generation of informers.

An intellectual circle, with bohemian pretensions and psychedelic experience, is being driven by the authorities without a murmur. In contrast to the 'chattering' intelligentsia, the silent generation is saying nothing about changes in the system. It is only their restless eyes, their anxiety, their nervous walk, the language of the market echoing through their coded speech, and my experience, the documents I have seen, which tell of changes that took place long ago.

The system in Russia has never changed, it was merely translated into its opposite when this became expedient. And people were content in the illusion that they had influence over the authorities. Then the population would weaken, and the state could work out new tactics to enslave them.

And the first generation to reach maturity in freedom, outside the system, is creating totalitarianism with its own hands, grounded in betrayal

Moscow 1996: young, free and out on the streets

and informing, with a new Gulag and millions of prisoners. The 'silent generation' will never ask 'why?' The silent generation merely signs records of judicial proceedings, with no change in its life or style between raves and raids from the militia. ❏

Alina Vitukhnovskaya is a poet and journalist living in Moscow. She was arrested in October 1994 and held for a year without trial on dubious drugs charges. Her case continues

Translated by Irena Maryniak

VÁCLAV HAVEL

A vote for nostalgia

Throughout eastern Europe, the Communists are on the return. Not in itself a cause for anxiety, says the president of the Czech Republic, more a matter of nostalgia, a proper democratic desire for change engendered by the harsh transition to the market

Charles Lambroschini *Six years after the fall of the Berlin Wall every election in eastern Europe is bringing victory to the ex-Communists, in Hungary, Lithuania, Bulgaria, Poland and finally in Russia. Does the return of Communists indicate the return of Communism?*

Václav Havel I don't think we need fear the return of Communism in countries where former Communists are back in power. Nobody wants to reinstate the old totalitarian system... Some representatives of parties formed by ex-Communists do feel nostalgic for the ancien régime, but many have made a full break with the past and are now straightforward social democrats, much like those in the West. One shouldn't put everyone in the same basket.

They have different policies on state intervention in the market economy and social policy. They may also have varying views on the scale of the business privatisation programme; but in the final analysis they have one thing in common: none want the restoration of old-style Communism.

I don't think that even in Russia the resurgence of Communism presents a threat, at least in the form that we knew it. The danger is the appearance of a more authoritarian power than we have come to expect in Europe. This form of government corresponds to time-honoured Russian traditions. If Communists in Russia are creating anxieties, it is less because of their conservative orientation than because of their tendency to think in terms of expansionism.

Among ex-Communists there are people who have considerable political experience, control over financial resources and agencies which they can rely on and who are accustomed, above all, to authoritarian collectivism, which is a more comfortable system of government. They have simply changed their colours and replaced Marxism with nationalism. With their populist rhetoric, these people seem to me to be particularly dangerous whether they are in the Balkans or the former Soviet republics. In many central European countries this danger is below the surface. If representatives of the West fail in their attempts to create a democratic order in the whole of Europe, and quickly, others will take matters into their own hands. Then it will be too late.

The western countries fought against Communism for decades, anticipating that it would be there for centuries. They did not expect such a speedy collapse. Nor were they adequately prepared for its consequences.

How do you explain the fact that people seem to have such short memories? Why are electors in central Europe as well as Russia already voting Communist?

In most cases one only has to remember that, over decades, people had grown accustomed to a paternalistic state which took care of their affairs and sometimes even thought for them. Now they can't get used to the radically new conditions created by the market economy and democracy. The explanation may also lie in the superior organisation of the Communist Party: it has succeeded in maintaining its organisational structures, its membership and financial means, allowing it to conduct a pre-election campaign more effectively than parties formed after the fall of Communism. Furthermore, one must not forget about the simple desire for change: eastern Europeans behave in the same way as electors in western Europe, where conservatives and social democrats alternate in power.

Have people grown weary of heroes? Even leaders of the dissident movement such as Solzhenitsyn, Walesa or Hável?

Quite right. Weariness has played its part. There are two explanations. First, dissidents were a minority, playing the role of a social conscience. And society always prefers to merge with the majority: with people who behave like everyone else, with those who have managed to swim to the surface. The same happened after the fall of Nazism in Germany and Austria. The anti-Fascist opposition fighters were praised, glorified. And then they were thrown out of political life, and returned only after many years...

Do you think that the turn-about to democracy made by Boris Yeltsin is genuine or simply prompted by the fact that the Soviet Union lost the Cold War?

President Yeltsin, despite his tendency towards a very authoritarian style of government, really does aspire to reform Russia...to lead his country down the irreversible road of democracy and market economics... Peter the Great also ruled with an iron hand while introducing numerous reforms... ❑

© *First published in* Figaro, *1996. Translated by Irena Maryniak*

IRENA MARYNIAK

Once and future leaders: Dudayev's supporters celebrate Independence Day in Grozny, 1995

Of blood and votes

**The result of the presidential election in June may be
determined less by Boris Yeltsin or Gennady Zyuganov than by
the direction of the new Chechen leadership**

THE reluctance of Russian politicians to recognise the rebel leader Dzhokhar Dudayev as a serious military and political opponent while he was alive has been matched only by their refusal publicly to acknowledge the real state of the Russian Federal Army. Now Dudayev is dead, reportedly killed in a rocket attack on the night of 21 April, and the blood feud which has long characterised relations between Russia and Chechnya can only be exacerbated.

Stories told by prominent Russian deputies, such as Yury Rybakov, who have visited the region and dodged army positions to talk to rebels, cannot easily be dismissed as 'negative reporting', in the way TV footage from Pervomayskoye was. The officially promoted distinction between Chechen fighters and the population at large is proving increasingly difficult to sustain. Following arbitrary massacres such as those in Sernovodsk or Samashki, civilians who have lost dozens of relatives are taking up arms. Children aged about 10 were seen shooting during the Chechen assault on Grozny on 6 March. Militiamen loyal to Moscow announced their refusal to fight Dudayev's men on local television. The March events in Grozny bore the hallmarks of a civilian insurrection. As Moscow's puppet president, Doku Zagayev, has confirmed, increasing numbers of Chechens are being drawn into the fighting.

The line that the war is being conducted by a few terrorist fighters has ceased to stand up. Today, an open trial for Dudayev's fellow commanders could prove more of an embarrassment for leading Russian politicians than their notion of public justice is worth. News of atrocities in an archipelago of Russian filtration camps has already seeped through to the West and the behaviour of the federal army has been denounced by independent human rights observers and the Organisation for Security and Co-operation in Europe (OSCE). At least 2,000 Chechen civilians have disappeared. In some cases ransoms of thousands of pounds have been paid to Russian troops. The allegations of atrocities, corruption and arms trafficking rebel leaders could, and likely would, make are bound to make Russian politicians pause. But Dudayev's death may open the floodgates to all those blood vendettas in which Caucasian history abounds.

The Chechen struggle against Russia goes back to imperial incursions into the Muslim region in the eighteenth century. Sporadic warfare has erupted whenever Russian control has weakened, and the long-standing grievance nursed by the Chechen against its imperial neighbour remains the rebels' most powerful weapon. It has demonstrated Russia's capacity for genocide for the second time this century; it has encouraged the Chechen people to rally round; it has radicalised and militarised the population. It has played on the Chechen tradition that values freedom, the martial ethos and loyalty to a chosen leader more highly than anything else. As Dudayev remarked when interviewed by journalist Oleg Moroz in 1992, the principle of the blood feud holds fast in Chechnya; the weapon is a symbol of potent manhood; summary justice for violent crime is assured.

According to the tenets of this tradition, Boris Yeltsin has long been any Chechen commander's blood enemy, and Dudayev was cast as avenger for the thousands of Chechens who have died. If it is not practicable to dispatch Yeltsin physically, the new rebel high command may yet find its way to doing so politically. Shortly before his death, Dudayev made remarks which indicated that he would not be averse to peace talks with a Communist leadership. His close supporter Akhmed Zakayev said that the Communists are the most 'serious' contenders in the forthcoming presidential election. Dudayev, once a Soviet air-force general, indicated that he never gave up his Party card and that he was against the original dissolution of the USSR — a statement well in line with the denunciation of the 1991 Bialowierza accords in the Communist-dominated Duma in March.

IT IS unlikely that the new rebel leadership can hope to secure full territorial independence from the Party that sanctioned the deportation of the Chechen people to Kazakhstan and Siberia in 1944. But any new presidency would doubtless seek to distance itself from the more disastrous mistakes of its predecessor. An agreement with the Communists, free of the burden of recent memories, could be a more serious proposition from the Chechen point of view than talks with Yeltsin.

Meanwhile, in the devastated towns and villages of Chechnya, Russian troops are undernourished and unpaid. The use of drugs and alcohol is widespread: a soldier here is more likely than not to be drunk or high. Famished conscripts are fed by Chechen villagers in exchange for safe passage. They are willing to ignore orders for a meal or a telephone call home. On International Women's Day, Russian soldiers reportedly shared a few drinks with Dudayev's men and subsequently sold them a tank and an armoured vehicle for US$6,000. The role of an occupation army, persistently under threat, triggers untold brutality towards civilians and suspicion or fear of the media whose function it is to expose Russia's military shame.

Back home, amid sporadic bouts of misinformation and censorship, Russian television has been showing the funerals of conscripts killed in and around Grozny — some, most recently, bombed by their own troops. The upsurge in fighting which preceded the announcement of President Yeltsin's peace initiative and the partial troop withdrawal on 31 March, may well have turned electors against Yeltsin. That was, perhaps, Dudayev's underlying intention and certainly the effect the president has since sought to counteract. Any further operations along the lines of the Grozny assault would bring the sight of more Russian losses to the television screens of countless families already resentful of Yeltsin's policies. This, together with the murder of hostages and prisoners of war or the threat of straightforward terrorism, remain strong cards in the hands of Chechen rebels if they fail to achieve the direct talks with Yeltsin which Dudayev demanded.

In the devastated towns and villages of Chechnya, Russian troops are undernourished and underpaid. The use of drugs and alcohol is widespread: a soldier is more likely than not to be drunk or high

As the Russian president comes to grips with his new image as peacemaker, Chechnya is being offered autonomy within the Russian Federation (along the lines agreed with Tatarstan). There has been mention of an amnesty for Chechen fighters other than those who have committed common-law crimes (presumably the hostage takers of Budennovsk and Pervomayskoye) and promise of better humanitarian aid and government funds for reconstruction. This, of course, is a particularly tall order in a country where all economic aid has a tendency to vanish and where billions of roubles regularly disappear in the course of salary distribution.

On a more spectacular scale, there has been talk of a grand bargain to settle all conflicts in the Caucasus, including Abkhazia, South Ossetia and Nagorno Karabakh; there has been an economic integration agreement with Kazakhstan, Kirgizia and Belarus; and discussions are underway on the passage of an oil pipeline from Baku on the Caspian Sea, through Azerbaijan up to Novorossiisk on the Black Sea — via Chechnya. Lack of

RAYISA AKHMATOVA

Poems from the Chechen Republic

Big is my hearth, wide is my table.
Perhaps my mother was not aware of a lot of things.
But if only I could weep now on her shoulder,
I would become stronger again.
Mother! Mother! Only you could understand,
without any proof or explanations,
how painful are the lies, how it hurts
to be in the midst of the battle of ambitions.
If only, in the dead of night,
I could speak to you without words,
all my pain would be relieved.
It is a dream, but then such fine and soul-healing dreams
could not be frightened away by all my sorrows.

★ ★

Like a freshly baked loaf of bread

progress on the status of the Black Sea fleet based in Sevastopol, on Ukrainian territory, remains a thorn in the flesh, but it all adds up to a last ditch attempt to present Boris Yeltsin as the democratic leader who preserved the integrity of the state against all the odds, not just within Russia's borders, but equally in the independent republics of the former Soviet Union.

Without a withdrawal from Chechnya, as Yeltsin himself has admitted, his chances of winning the presidential election are minimal. He has remained ambivalently committed to a solution which combines hard military and judicial rhetoric with as much peacemaking as pride will allow. 'It is above all a peace programme,' he has said. 'Second, it is a military programme. The criminals responsible for and implicated in terrorism must stand trial. Others must learn the lesson.'

Rebel leaders are unimpressed. General Vyacheslav Tikhomorov, the Russian commander in Chechnya, and General Alexander Lebed, another

our coat of arms ascended above the mountains,
joyfully shining on us from above...
And above the peaks our banner soared
like the first poppies on the mountains.

★ ★

What should I wish to you, my son,
at the beginning of your destiny?
Only the same you'd in turn wish to your own son.

What gift should I give to you, my son,
at the beginning of the tangled roads?
Only the same you'd in turn give your own son.

Being your mother I am your father as well.
I have to guide you and wish you well.
But, alas you have already become a man.

Rayisa Akhmatova *is among Chechnya's best-known poets*

Translated by Ravil Bukharaev

contender for the presidency, have said that a halt to military operations cannot be quickly implemented. It will take a great deal of determination to prevent the initiative from going the way of last summer's failed ceasefire. As some troops retire to the borders of Chechnya, reactions in Dagestan and Ingushetia to the prospect of an indefinite, battle-hardened military presence on their territory could be decisive.

Meanwhile, opinion polls continue to show that the Russian population is more deeply concerned about the Chechen débâcle than about poor living standards or organised crime. The 18-month-old conflict has cost an estimated 40,000 lives and created at least 250,000 refugees. It is a sorry tale of political paradox and misjudgement. And its legacy could cost still more, as Boris Yeltsin dons the mantle of peacemaker to salvage an election, and Chechen rebel leaders demand his moral capitulation and continue to woo the Russian people — by killing them. ❑

RAVIL BUKHARAEV & BILAL MAMBET

Russia's other people

A BOUt 100 ethnic groups live on the territory of the Russian Federation, speaking about 150 languages between them. The Russians are in the majority (an estimated 81.5 per cent of the population) in all but three regions of the country: the northern slopes of the Caucasus, the Ural Mountains with their west-flowing rivers, and Eastern Siberia (the Yakut, Buryat and Tuvinian autonomous republics).

In the northern Caucasus the Chechen have sought, since the collapse of the Soviet Union, to break with Russia and establish an independent state. It is less well known that the Tatars (the second biggest ethnic group in Russia) have made gestures in the same direction.

The republic of Tatarstan, just west of the Urals, contains an estimated 1.7 million Tatars, about 26 per cent of the entire Tatar population of Russia. One distinct Tatar community of about 500,000 lived in the Crimea from the thirteenth century, but was brutally deported to the Urals, Siberia and Central Asia in 1945 for alleged collaboration with the Nazis. A minority have since been allowed to return home. Most remain in Uzbekistan and other parts of Central Asia. Like Chechnya, Tatarstan refused to sign the 1992 Federation Treaty with Moscow. Since then, its leadership has succeeded in charting an independent course for the republic without unduly alienating the centre. **IM**

RAVIL BUKHARAEV

Civil despair

It got dark at midday, in the sky and in me.
A little rain fell on my open book.
The smoothed raws of the spring lindens
lay like shadows on the ground.
Moving positions, the links
of customary imaginations and worries broke,
a tattered petal of the sweetbriar
fell in the dark whirlpool of inspiration.

But this is all unclear. I will forget everything:
the movement of shadows, the sweetbriar, the lindens,
the slow squeaks of the wet bench,

the round edges of the clouds,
the pages illuminated by rays
and the white stripes on the asphalt,
but not the poems on civil themes,
the poems of civil despair.

Ravil Bukharaev is a UK-based Tatar poet writing in English, Russian, Tatar and Hungarian

Translated by Richard McKane

BILAL MAMBET

Thinking of the homeland

My homeland!
Everything here's covered in mist.
Where does this fog come from,
those woods, meadows or mountains?
If it was rising from the earth of the homeland,
I would recognise it at once.

Everything changes shape and floats —
the rows of fruit trees,
the long meadows...

The expanse of the faraway fields strikes my eyes,
is it not sufficient to satisfy their hunger?

These roads of stone call me to hit the road again,
though friendly souls sometimes comfort my anguish.
The guest who has come — has to return home.
Next time which land shall I call my homeland?

Bilal Mambet is a Crimean Tatar poet based in Sevastapol

Translated by Ravil Bukharaev

GEOFFREY KEELING

VIKTOR PELEVIN

Astrakhan on the Kremlin towers

SINCE the age of Homer there has been an extraordinary persistence about his theme of one group of heroes defending a fortress while another is trying to storm it. Embarrassingly inappropriate examples can be found by opening any newspaper and reading, say, about 'the storming of the cosmos'. Let us not be thrown by the fact that what is being stormed in this instance is a void, but rather see it as further confirmation of the thesis of the philosopher Ilyin that Russian thought evolves inexorably to an instinctive buddhism.

It is interesting, and indeed instructive, that the identity of the defenders seems never to be very clear, perhaps because the assaults seem never to succeed fully. Even more interesting is the fact that where an event in real life fits perfectly into Homer's framework, our consciousness will refuse categorically to acknowledge any resemblance. The defenders themselves are rarely even aware that they have defended a fortress, as our story will demonstrate.

For some reason, that memorable August day when the Kremlin was stormed by the Chechen leader Shamil Basayev, news of its fall proved strangely reluctant to cross the boundary of Moscow's inner ring road. Perhaps talk of its 'fall' seemed incongruous when the operation had been accomplished without bloodshed (if we overlook the wasting of the traffic policeman perched in a glass tumbler at the entrance to the Kremlin. Even there, as was later established, he was shot only because the female Ukrainian sniper in one of the leading vehicles overreacted to the suspiciously large black telephone into which he was talking.) The lightning success of the operation was doubtless due primarily to meticulous planning, and to lessons having been learnt from the Budennovsk raid.

This time there were no trucks and no camouflage. Two hundred men of Basayev's assault and sabotage battalion travelled up to Moscow in 40 Mercedes 600s requisitioned from inhabitants of the mountainous regions of Chechnya. The successful outcome was due in part to the fact that most of the vehicles were equipped, in accordance with the mountain-dwellers' etiquette, with emergency vehicle flashing lights. Each of the battalion's fighters was clean shaven and wore a cheerful maroon blazer (hastily fashioned from sacks dyed with beetroot juice), and around their necks a heavy gold(-painted toilet) chain. These, as the subsequent commission of enquiry was to establish, had been put through as a rush order by one of the Grozny funeral parlours.

In accordance with the initial operational plan all the Kremlin's entrances and exits were immediately barricaded. Weapons stockpiled in advance were retrieved from the cellars of the Palace of Congresses, the fighters changed back into their traditional combat jackets, and the telescopic sights of Basayev's snipers were soon glinting from the Kremlin battlements. The assault had been a complete success, except that not a single member of the government, or even a civil servant of any distinction, had been seized. In all, Basayev's men had taken some 20 hostages, mostly employees of the casino in the Palace of Congresses, along with a few fitters engaged in maintenance work despite its being a Sunday. Basayev was not in the least put out by this modest haul.

'They come by themselves tomorrow, trast me,' he said to his distraught Pakistani adviser. 'So many we can't keep them all in prison.'

The terrorist leader's intuition did not fail him, but of this more anon. Immediately after occupying the Kremlin and organising defensive positions on the three main axes along which counter-attacks were to be expected, Shamil Basayev proceeded to implement the second part of his plan. This related directly to a phenomenon which might at first sight seem remote from terrorism, namely the steep rise in the price of Astrakhan fleeces on the Moscow fur exchange. Picking up the telephone, Basayev dialled a number which he knew by heart, uttered a single codeword, and rang off.

Nowadays we all know that behind bloodshed there is always somebody's money. Shamil Basayev's activities were no exception. It has now been established beyond doubt that Basayev's principal sponsor and ally in Moscow was the chairman of the Aenea Bank, Kim Polkanov. He it was who a good two months before the events described had engaged in intensive speculative buying of Astrakhan fleeces which, in consequence, almost trebled in price.

The Aenea Bank took its name from Polkanov's method of accumulating his start-up capital. He would hang a sign bearing the legend 'Bureau de Change' at the entrance to a dark alleyway and when a customer appeared asking where the bank was he would reply 'In 'ere' and strike him a sharp blow with a hammer kept for the purpose.

Immediately after the phone call two covered trucks drove out from Polkanov's dacha and headed for the Kremlin, which they entered unhindered. The gates were at once closed behind them, and a few hours later the red stars on the towers of the Kremlin disappeared beneath gigantic Astrakhan fur hats.

Basayev's men who carried out this operation had undergone a lengthy period of training in the mountains of Chechnya. Ordering the sentries to redouble their vigilance, Basayev said *namaz* and awaited the appearance of mediators.

His wait was a lengthy one. As we have already noted, for a considerable time rumours that the Kremlin had been seized circulated only within the confines of the inner ring road, spread in the main by taxi-drivers who refused to carry passengers through the city centre, or demanded improbably high fares to do so. The Federal Security Service (FSS) first heard of the terrorists' success from one of their employees who had tried to take a taxi to work. They didn't take it seriously at first, but decided to check it out with the Moscow office of CNN, who advised that nothing had been synchronised with them, from which the FSS concluded that the whole thing was a hoax.

The situation was further complicated by the fact that all the top FSS brass were away accompanying the president, who was inflicting an official visit on Greenland, which left nobody at home with authority to take rapid decisions. No credence should be given to assertions that the president's bodyguards had been tipped off and simply carted their meal ticket as far as possible out of harm's way. This is manifestly scabrous pre-election rumour-mongering. Neither do we consider it necessary to refute the allegation that the remote location chosen for the presidential visit had anything to do with the terrorists' having picked up an atomic warhead on the cheap during their progress through the Ukraine.

When, however, the authorities were finally persuaded that Basayev had indeed seized the Kremlin, the analysts of the FSS were instructed to propose appropriate counter-measures. As a first priority it was deemed essential to give the inhabitants of the capital an explanation for the appearance of the enormous Astrakhan fur hats on the towers of the Kremlin (although, if we are to be entirely honest, very few people had actually noticed them). To this end disinformation was spread through the city and over a number of subordinate television channels to the effect that a concert would be taking place in Red Square at which Makhmud Esembayev would be accompanied by a group of Sufi musicians who were flying in from Pakistan. It was even claimed that the event was being sponsored by Peter Gabriel, and that Nushrat Fatekh Ali-Khan would be singing with Esembayev. Immediately after this announcement a huge quantity of undated tickets were printed and sold in Moscow by persons unknown.

The Kremlin was cordoned off and closed to visitors, but this evoked no surprise. The Russian people continued, as it had since Pushkin penned the last scene of *Boris Godunov*, to keep its counsel. Negotiations were conducted with Basayev over police frequencies. He had settled into the bunker under the Palace of Congresses and his demands which, according to confidential information, related to the granting of vast loans to revive farming in Chechnya, had already virtually been conceded. It might have been possible to conceal the seizure of the Kremlin entirely had not a number of Basayev's men started trading grenade launchers and ammunition in Alexander Park right next to the Kremlin walls. When rival arms traders from a certain location on Kotelnicheskaya Embankment heard of this and sent round their heavies to sort them out, Basayev's men simply locked themselves in the Kremlin. The incident came to the attention of journalists, and ended all further possibility of concealing the occupation.

The FSS now decided to resort to force, but the Alpha special forces group's reaction to the suggestion that they should storm the Kremlin while taking care not to cause any damage was extremely rude, and it was decided instead to pressure the terrorists indirectly by cutting off their water, light, and sanitation. However, after several grenades were launched from behind the walls and a caustic remark was made in a newspaper controlled by Polkanov's Bank that only the present Russian government was capable of treating unknown bandits the same way as it treated legitimately elected members of parliament, mains water and sanitation were restored.

Press reaction was varied, but some of the more intellectual newspapers remarked coyly on a certain resemblance of the Astrakhan caps to condoms and wrote about the inevitability in the post-imperial era of a demasculinisation of the Kremlin, an Oedipus complex among the newly independent former Soviet republics with regard to their former mother country, and much else besides. Indeed, the level of insight in such articles was of such a high order that one could scarcely imagine how an event like the seizing of the Kremlin was possible in a country inhabited by such clever people. The ultra-patriotic press achieved a rare degree of unanimity. Since, they contended, it is indisputable that the Kremlin is controlled by Jews, and since Basayev has occupied the Kremlin and consequently controls it, no further doubt can remain as to his racial origins. Basayev was simply a run-of-the-mill agent of international Zionism and was acting on the orders of its world government. A number of intriguing facts about his biography were made public, including a dozen or so variants of his real surname, which ranged from Basaiman to Gorgonzoller. Some sources claim that the latter surname was not unrelated to an inferior pizza served to the patriotic journalist concerned in the Chechen pizzeria on Gorky Street. The ultra-right journalists were, however, all agreed that his real first name was Schlemihl.

Meanwhile Basayev's prediction about volunteer hostages began to be realised. The Borovitsky Gate was opened to admit them. In the first two days the influx was so large that the terrorists guarding the entrance had to arrange a small vetting station by the gate, allowing into the Kremlin only television reporters and celebrities of one kind or another: society gurus, variety artistes, members of parliament, television presenters, and anyone else who might add to the publicity value of Basayev's performance.

The opening of the Borovitsky Gate for the admission of hostages and television crews was, however, the moment when the first crack, as yet invisible, opened in the ground beneath Basayev's feet. This, to paraphrase the immortal words of Winston Churchill, was the beginning of the end.

It would be unfair to say that Basayev had committed an error which was to wreck the entire operation. It was later claimed in numerous interviews that he had been defeated by Operation Trojan Horse, but in fact at the moment when the mass inflow of hostages to the Kremlin began the FSS was in a state of total paralysis. Virtually the entire beau monde of the capital had presented itself. A demonstration on Manège Square by several dozen patriots waving banners reading 'Arrest the Gorgonzoller Gang' had to be dispersed because it was interfering with the televising of the arrival of more and more celebrity hostages. Many came with a variety of home comforts, sandwiches and thermos flasks and regaled the ravenous fighters, so that the Kremlin events began to take on the aspect of an enormous family picnic.

But then, taking advantage of the attentive television lenses glinting from every corner, the hostages assembled in the Kremlin gradually proceeded to what it was they had actually come for.

It all started when the renowned vocalist Polyp Pigdick succeeded in becoming the centre of attention. Disporting himself in front of the cameras for some time in his saffron cloak and green turban, he suddenly pointed skywards in amazement and collapsed in what appeared to be a fainting fit. When those around him looked up they discovered that a trapeze had been suspended at a dizzying height between the towers on which his celebrated friend Stepanida Razina was flying back and forth illuminated by spotlights. A microphone materialised in Pigdick's hands and, with much expressive play of the eyebrows, he began to sing,

'Do not believe them when they say
The Kremlin path is one of ease!'

As he sang, he gazed in an agony of plaintive languor at the corpulent Stepanida cleaving the night sky high above and stretched out his hand to her, clearly giving those present to understand that he was singing for her alone.

This had the effect of a starting pistol on all those assembled. Almost immediately in another corner of the Kremlin dazzling arc lights came on and a twisted figure with a red beard and close-set beady eyes who had been one of the first to volunteer himself as a hostage began filming an advertising video for Adidas trainers, with the participation of a number of Chechens hired for very large fees. The concept was unsophisticated: gunfire in the night, tracer bullets, a glimpse of masked faces, soft cat-like leaping in the dark. Somebody stumbles and does not rise, and the last shot shows feet in Adidas trainers, lit by a flare, the bearded face of a vanquished foe and the smoking barrel of a semi-automatic rifle. There followed a niftily edited sequence: three rifle muzzles bound with insulating tape, the three stripes on the trainers, three flares in the sky. This was the first video to use the new slogan, specially devised for the countries of the CIS: 'Adidas. The bitter joy of victory!' (later superseded by: 'Adidas. Three on the side and you're dead.')

At the same time another film crew were rolling the first trials for a change of image for the smoker of Winston high tar cigarettes to determine whether the whiskered outdoor hero should be replaced by a bearded figure in combat kit, and the ember from the campfire by a lit Molotov cocktail.

In short order Basayev found himself and his thugs sidelined, and when he tried to put a stop to what he called debauchery and immorality, giving orders that all filming was to stop and that the hostages and television crews were to be locked up in the Kremlin Palace of Congresses, he was unexpectedly detached from the handful of fighters not yet employed by film crews and politely advised that he wasn't in Budennovsk now and he'd better cool it if he didn't want to find himself wearing concrete boots at the bottom of the Moscow River.

Shocked by such unprecedented disrespect, Basayev turned to his Pakistani advisers, who contacted their Moscow residency using the secure Kremlin telephone system. Basayev was horrified to discover that advertising slots between reports from the Kremlin were running at a full US$250,000 a minute. An hour-long news programme titled *Astrakhan on the Kremlin Towers* was scheduled for broadcast every evening, and had been written into the Ostankino broadcasting schedules for a month ahead. Thirty minutes of the hour were allocated to advertising.

Basayev soon recognised that while his assault and sabotage battalion might successfully resist a couple of armoured tank divisions of the Russian army, it was certainly no match for that kind of money. The moral fibre of his fighters was being undermined at a phenomenal rate. Many had succumbed, and begun drinking and consorting with women, a great many of whom were now gathered in the Kremlin in anticipation of the 'Legs and Smoke' beauty contest. When Basayev tried to find out how all these people had got in, he discovered that control of admissions through the Borovitsky Gate had gradually and in a wholly opaque manner passed from his deputy for religious matters Khodzhi Akhundov to an Armenian called Eddie Simonyan, and that quite apart from group bookings like the beauty contest, anybody with US$5,000 to spare was free to enter.

Working out that the admission price for an assault on the Kremlin would be well beyond the means of the Russian army, Basayev was somewhat reassured. The following morning, however, he was approached by a major television producer who glanced anxiously at the two grenade launchers Shamil, who happened to be in a bad mood that day, had hung about his person, and said,

'Mr er — em Basayev, forgive my troubling you, I know you are a busy man, but you will understand, we have put big, very big money in here, and there are some very odd characters sloping around. Could you tighten up admissions procedures, do you think? We have the élite of Russian culture here. Imagine what might happen if a group of terrorists were to get in...'

This was the moment when Shamil was forced to recognise that the situation was out of control. It was not only the nightly programme *Astrakhan on the Kremlin Towers*. Advertising rates for all news programmes had doubled. He decided to withdraw in total secrecy. He therefore contacted the FSS and demanded two trucks and five million dollars, calculating that this should be sufficient to bribe the traffic police all the way back to the northern Caucasus.

The forces loyal to Basayev were by now down to eight or nine diehards. One night he and his remaining fighters piled into two Mercedes and, under the pretext of inspecting his guards, slipped out of the Kremlin. The terrorists' last victim was that well-known avant-gardiste Shura Brenny who, in the presence of a large crowd, was masturbating with the aid of a grenade launcher directly in the path of the fighters. The female Ukrainian sniper who shot him had overreacted to the suspiciously large black telephone on which Shura was about to ejaculate in the cause of art. If this minor incident is ignored, the evacuation took place without incident. Basayev was silent the whole way, but when his vehicle stopped at the ring road where he and his people were to transfer to the trucks he turned, as the few people present later recalled, to face Moscow, raised his fist to the firmament (which was turning pink in the first rays of dawn), shook it and shouted,

'Woe to thee, Babylon, that great city!'

They say tears started to his eyes. Need we add that in Basayev's last words, which very soon became public knowledge, the patriotic press found final, incontrovertible proof of his Jewish origins.

If at the end of our brief narrative we return to where we began, namely the mythical storming of a fortress, then the position of those doing the storming seems straightforward enough. What is less clear is who was defending it. Are we really to say that Moscow was saved by Polyp Pigdick? And yet, to the unbiased eye, that would seem to have been the case. The events taking place in Russia seem explicable only in terms of Lobachevskian logic, and their meaning, if there is one, only discoverable from a great distance in time.

Or to put it another way: Russia's history is a kind of fourth dimension of its chronology, and only when you look out from this fourth dimension do all the inexplicably monstrous shifts and zigzags and shudders of her day-to-day existence merge into a clear, distinct line, straight as an arrow. ❏

Victor Pelevin is the brightest of Russia's new writers and has a developed sense of (black) humour. Several of his stories are published in English translation in Glas New Russian Writing, *No 4 (1993) and No 7 (1994) and his novellas* Omon Ra, The Yellow Arrow, *and* The Life of the Insects *are published by Harbord Press, London*

First published in Russian in Ogonyok No 42, 1995
Translated by Arch Tait

Staying alive

'Are you staying or going?'

'I'm staying. I'm staying at least until I need to go. And probably when I'm fed up to the back teeth with it. But at the moment I want to stay, I like this country. I like the people, they're very warm people, at the same time there's a very real feeling of living out here. And the Russians understand what it is to be alive. Maybe because most of the country is on the poverty line, close to starvation, or sickness or death — these things are translated into quite a fatalistic mentality, and to quite an appreciation of living. And you've got to realise that in this country the average life expectancy for a man is 55 years old. And for a woman, 60. People don't live very long in this country. Out here, it's a whole new ball game.'

Excerpted from 'Bucks in the USSR', BBC Radio 4

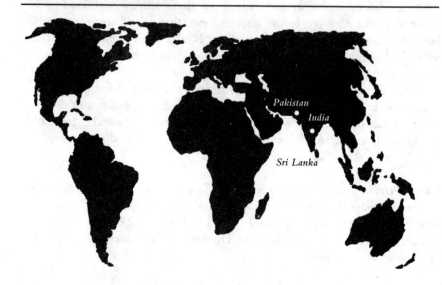

A testing time for democracy

INDIA, the world's most populous democratic state, goes to the polls in April and May. An estimated 590 million people are eligible to give their verdict on five years of Narasimha Rao's administration. It is a massive exercise, with voting on six separate days over the course of a month.

Taken at face value the election is effectively a referendum on Rao's programme of economic liberalisation, which has done a lot for India's small professional class — the Bombay stock exchange is currently booming on the back of foreign investment, despite the threat of political instability — but has made little improvement to the lives of the lower castes and religious minorities who together account for some 85 per cent of the population. Rao's campaign slogan — 'you give me stability, I will give you prosperity' — is a tacit admission of the deep communal, ethnic, regional and religious fissures in Indian society.

Rao's Congress party is itself split down the middle over the massive corruption scandal which broke in January, seriously jeopardising his chances of re-election. The rival Hindu nationalist Bharatiya Janata Party (BJP) is unlikely to muster enough support nationally to form a government outright. This means the various regional parties, factional groupings within the Lok Sabha (the lower house of Parliament) and the Left Front-National Front alliance will almost certainly be jockeying for the balance of power, in a sectarian alliance that could spell trouble for minorities — such as the 110 million-strong Muslim community. Historically, non-Congress governments have an extremely short life-expectancy. Come the end of May, and stability could well be at a premium in India.

In Pakistan, ongoing conflict between the Mohajir Quami Movement (MQM) and the state security forces has left the streets of Karachi drenched in blood (*Index* 4/1995, p23). One point at issue is the extent to which the Mohajirs — migrants from India — should exercise political and cultural autonomy in Karachi, where they are in the majority. A recent measure, to reduce still further the powers of the Karachi Metropolitan Corporation in favour of the Sindh provincial government — from which all the MQM's members have now been forcibly excluded — can only inflame matters. With each side blaming the other for the worst excesses of violence, the Bhutto government's offer of local elections in exchange for a minimum three-month MQM ceasefire looks disingenuous, to say the least.

And in Sri Lanka, Tamil separatists and government forces have spent 13 years and killed 50,000 people between them in a struggle for control of the north and east of the island. Now the government has invoked new emergency powers to postpone the local government elections which were scheduled for June, because, they say, the army is too busy fighting the Tamil Tigers to guarantee an orderly vote. Further, they have slapped an absolute ban on local media from carrying any coverage of the army's latest offensive against the guerrillas.

India, meanwhile, has its own separatist war going on in Jammu and Kashmir. With only six members returned to the 543-member Lok Sabha, the province won't have an enormous effect on the outcome of the elections, but the government has assigned 230,000 troops to keep the peace during the voting period. The Hizbul Mujahideen have sworn to undermine the process and have warned that government officials can expect 'severe consequences' for facilitating the vote.

At its most basic, a democratic system is meant to provide a decision-making mechanism, within which intractable and fundamental political conflicts can be addressed and resolved without recourse to violence — ballots instead of bullets. Time and again, however, the subcontinent's democracies have signally failed to deliver. India's time of reckoning is nigh. ❑

Adam Newey

A censorship chronicle incorporating information from Agence France-Presse (AFP), the American Association for the Advancement of Science Human Rights Action Network (AAASHRAN), Amnesty International (AI), Article 19 (A19), the BBC Monitoring Service Summary of World Broadcasts (SWB), the Committee to Protect Journalists (CPJ), the Canadian Committee to Protect Journalists (CCPJ), the Inter-American Press Association (IAPA), the International Federation of Journalists (IFJ/FIP), Human Rights Watch (HRW), the Media Institute of Southern Africa (MISA), International PEN (PEN), Open Media Research Institute (OMRI), Reporters Sans Frontières (RSF), the World Association of Community Broadcasters (AMARC) and other sources

ALBANIA

In early February the Constitutional Court overturned those clauses of the **Law on Verification of Moral Stature** (*Index* 1/1996) banning former Sigurimi collaborators from working at any newspaper with a daily circulation over 3,000. (HRW)

Historian **Elvira Shapllo**, archaeologist **Vladimir Qiriaqi**, artist **Jani Bardho** and businessman **Thoma Ngjelo** went on trial in Gjirokaster in February accused of 'distributing anti-constitutional writings'. They are authors of a guidebook to Gjirokaster which contained a picture of ex-dictator Enver Hoxha, a native of the town. The trial is

reported to have been adjourned. (AI)

Blendi Fevziu (*Index* 1/1996), editor-in-chief of *Aleanca*, was assaulted by two people on 12 February, apparently in connection with an article he published about former Communists. (IFJ)

On 26 February, followng a fatal car bomb in Tirana, state television suggested a link between the bomb and an article by **Ylli Polovina** published in *Populli Po* in November 1995, which suggested that bombings such as the one that injured Macedonian president Koro Gligorov could happen in Albania. Polovina was arrested and later charged with 'inciting terrorism'. He was convicted and fined US$300. Also on 26 February police raided the offices of *Koha Jone* and arrested all present, including the office cleaner. They were questioned about the car bomb. Observers believe the explosion was used as a pretext for arbitrary action against the independent press. (IFJ, Article 19, Reuter, *Albanian Daily News*)

Activists **Sami Meta, Kritaq Mosko, Timoshenko Pekmezi** and **Tare Isufi** were arrested in Tirana on 1 March on charges of 'creating anti-constitutional parties and associations', an offence punishable by one to five years in prison. After reports that Communist tracts had been distributed in Tirana they were accused of 'recreating' the outlawed Communist Party. All except Isufi remain in custody. And on 21 March

Dilaver Dauti, Lirim Veliu, Gani Koro and **Sulejman Mejkollari** were found guilty of distributing 'anti-constitutional' leaflets. Mejkollari was also found guilty of 'recreating' the Communist Party and sentenced to four years in jail. Dauti and Veliu received prison terms of two years and six months respectively. Koro received three years' probation. (SWB, AI)

Kristo Mertiri, deputy chief editor of *Kombi*, was fined US$1,000 on 4 March after a Tirana court found him guilty of defaming the secret police. (Reuter, *Zeri i Popullit*)

On 8 March *Koha Jone* reported that the Supreme Court has turned down for the third time a request for permission to found a Democratic Islamic Union Party, asking that details be furnished as to the religious implications of the name. (Reuter)

Arban Hasani, former editor-in-chief of *Populli Po*, was fined US$1,000 for publishing an article implicating Kosovo Albanians in drug smuggling and prostitution on 12 March. He also faces trial in a separate case over complaints that he wrongly reported that a Shkoder policeman had accused the SHIK secret police of involvement in the killing of a local politician. (IFJ, OMRI)

On 14 March **Aleksander Frangaj**, editor-in-chief of *Koha Jone*, was fined for publishing 'false reports' in relation to a 1994 article on the Albanian secret service. Under

Albanian law chief editors and publishers are accountable for articles containing false information. On 16 March **Aleko Likaj**, a *Koha Jone* journalist, was attacked by three people over an article he had written about the closure of a gaming house. (IFJ, OMRI)

Recent publication: *Human Rights in Post-Communist Albania* (HRW/Helsinki, 1996, 156pp)

ALGERIA

The 4 March edition of the French-language weekly *La Nation* was seized at the printing presses to prevent publication of an in-depth investigation into human rights abuses committed by the government (*see p177*). The 25 March edition was also seized at the printing presses by the Interior Ministry, allegedly because it contained 'an apology for terrorism'. And on the night of 7-8 April the Arabic-language *El Houria*, owned by the same private company as *La Nation*, was confiscated at the printing presses in connection with an article on political assassinations. (Reuter, RSF)

Djilali Arabdiou, a photojournalist for *Algérie Actualité*, was shot dead as he left his home in Algiers on 12 March. (*Guardian*)

Official accreditation of *El Pais*'s Algiers correspondent **Ferran Sales** was withdrawn on 24 March, effectively closing the Spanish daily's bureau in Algeria. The foreign ministry's press chief

reportedly told Sales that the government did not like his reporting. (*Independent*)

A visit planned for 29 March by representatives from the International Federation of Journalists (IFJ) and the International Federation of Newspaper Publishers (FIEJ) was cancelled at short notice by the Algerian authorities. The two organisations have launched a campaign to support independent media in Algeria and provide practical assistance to three newspapers whose offices were destroyed in a bomb attack in February (*Index* 2/1996). No reason for the cancellation was given. (IFJ)

Omar Belhouchet, editor-in-chief of the daily *El Watan*, was charged with contempt on 14 April in connection with an article criticising Zoubir Sifi, brother of the former prime minister. He was released on bail. (RSF)

ARGENTINA

On 22 March police went to the offices of the *Buenos Aires Herald* with an arrest warrant for **Jacobo Timerman** on charges of libel. The newspaper is the provisional address of the journalists' organisation **Periodistas**, of which Timerman — one of Argentina's most respected journalists — is a founding member. The warrant stems from libel charges brought against Timerman by President Menem in 1988, and of which he was acquitted in two separate trials. However, the Supreme Court reopened the case 18 months ago at Menem's request. (CPJ)

AZERBAIJAN

Azer Gusseinbala, parliamentary correspondent for the opposition paper *Azadlyg*, and **Taptig Farhadoglu** of the independent news agency *Turan*, were stripped of their parliamentary accreditation in mid-March, shortly after Djalal Aliev, President Aliev's brother, accused the opposition press of 'provocation and hooliganism' and said they should not be tolerated in Parliament. (RSF)

On 10 April the daily *Muhalifat* printed the text of an appeal, reportedly written in human blood, by a member of the OPON special police imprisoned for his part in last year's confrontation with government troops. The paper's staff may face official sanction for failing to submit the text to the government censor in advance. (OMRI)

BAHRAIN

On 24 February a bomb exploded in Manama, in front of the office of *al-Ayam*, a privately owned, pro-government daily. The explosion destroyed the car of the editor-in-chief, Nabil al-Hammar. According to one report, an employee in the paper's library was wounded by the explosion. The paper received an anonymous call after the explosion claiming responsibility, and connecting the bomb with *al-Ayam*'s publication of the photos of four suspects arrested by police for the bombing of two hotels and a commercial centre. (CPJ)

A first for Algeria
by Salima Ghezali

I BECAME editor of *La Nation* in 1993 at a moment when many journalists had been killed and most senior journalists had fled. The authorities claimed about 40-50 journalists had been assassinated by the Islamist groups, mainly those writing in French and expressing radical, anti-Islamist opinions. Later, all journalists, even those writing in Arabic, became targets and many have been killed.

In wartime, women can assume high positions because they're dangerous. If it weren't for the war, I think a lot of men would have said, 'No, no, no! She can't do that.' Today, to be a journalist, to be an editor-in-chief, particularly since our paper condemns both sides in the war, needs strength. I think I've got it.

La Nation's dossier on human rights covered violations by government authorities (*see page 177*). It was the first time journalists wrote about attempted assassinations by the authorities, about deaths in jail, about 'disappearances': the first time we've spoken about real conditions and the injustice in Algeria. In the past, newspapers have only written about the atrocities committed by the armed Islamist groups, not by the government itself.

So they stopped the newspaper: there was a communique from the minister of the interior claiming we were supporting terrorism.

Our dossier was important because people had no idea that the government was involved in such things; didn't understand why, for example, there was a problem in opening negotiations with the opposition, including the Islamists. The government says the opposition must condemn violence, terrorism and then they'll begin negotiations. The opposition says, 'Sure. But you must be willing to condemn *all* acts of violence.' To which the government responds by saying there is only one [source of] violence. We can't stop the war if we don't recognise this.

We have an authoritarian tradition here that reaches deep into society and into the

The trial of writer and activist **Ahmad al-Shamlan** (*Index* 2/1996) on charges of endangering national security was adjourned in April to give the defence time to consider the evidence against him. Freelance journalist **Mahdi Rabea** also went on trial in early April for 'possessing and disseminating literature containing false news aimed at destabilising national security' by drafting opposition leaflets. Rabea says he has been tortured in detention. (PEN)

BANGLADESH

Over 10,000 people associated with opposition parties were reportedly arrested without warrant during the run-up to the 15 February parliamentary election in what the security forces claimed was a crackdown on unauthorised weapons. Security forces have been accused of beating and torturing detainees. After the election, which was boycotted by the opposition, at least 14 people were killed during strikes and street battles as the opposition campaigned to force prime minister Khaleda Zia to resign. Police acknowledge that by 31 March at least 120 people had died and thousands more been injured. Violence has continued after Khaleda's resignation at the end of March, which sparks fresh elections before the end of June. The caretaker government overseeing the new election sacked the head of state-owned Bangladesh minds of individuals. You have to choose your camp. If you choose neither, or condemn both, it's not easy. I've received death threats, it happens all the time, it's banal. Or someone calls you, you don't know who it is. Sometimes...I can't sleep at night but I'm in charge here and I have to be stronger than the others. There are so many people with weapons, such chaos: anyone can come and kill you and the government will simply say, 'Ah, there go the terrorists.'

We must look for a political solution. The government must accept the idea that we have to open negotiations with the opposition. The opposition recently proposed this to President Liamine Zeroual, but he refused. And now, if he continues to refuse, if they close the political channels again, the violence will continue to escalate. The government's responsibility is great.

At the time of the presidential elections last November, *La Nation* tried to say what millions of Algerians say every day: stop the war; begin negotiations; we want to live in peace; we don't want to destroy our country. The Algerians who voted said they were voting for peace. But the authorities are criminal: all the elements for an end to the war are there, but they don't want that. There is a minority of extremist groups who will not accept negotiations, who don't want things to be normal again. All the others want peace and the government refuses.

We must make people believe that with freedom of expression democracy is protected. Since the war of liberation, people have believed in violence as a solution and, at the end of the day, they risk supporting the argument of the Islamists.

Only God knows what will happen when I get back to Algeria. But I'll carry on as usual. The government will continue in its way and we in ours. They try to keep us down and, from time to time, succeed; whenever there's an opportunity to say something, we'll say it. It's important to know your conscience is clear and that you can live with your conscience.

Interviewed in London by **Julie Wheelwright**, *a freelance journalist specialising in the Middle East*

Television (BTV), **Risalat Ahmed**, on 17 April after opposition parties complained that the station was biased towards Khaleda's Bangladesh Nationalist Party. (Reuter, AI)

Mohammad Quaruzzaman, a journalist with *Neel Sagar*, was shot dead on 19 February by police firing on supporters of a Bangladesh National Party (BNP) candidate. Police reportedly kicked and beat Quaruzzaman as he lay dying on the ground. On 27

February police arrested **Syed Borhan Kabir**, chief reporter with *Ajker Kagoj*, after Kabir's reports on the crisis had angered the authorities. The home and office of **Kazi Shahed Ahmed**, the paper's editor, were also raided. **Anwar Hossain Monju**, editor of *Ittefaq*, was jailed on 24 February, and **Alhaj Mokbul Hossain**, editor of *al-Ameen*, was jailed on 12 February, both under the 30-day detention provisions of the 1974 Special Powers Act. At

least six journalists were injured by police on 24 February: **Jasim Ahmed** and **Azmal Huq** of *Rupali*, **Alam Masud** and **Shahidul Islam** of *Desh Janata*, **Kazi Borhanuddin** of *Banglabazar* and **Salimullah Selim** of *Shakaler Khabar* were clubbed while covering the arrest of opposition MP Motia Chowdhury. (Reuter, RSF)

BELARUS

On 20 March **Nikolai Galko**,

editor of the leading daily *Narodnaya Gazeta*, was fired by President Lukashenka for criticising the president and the state of the media in general. Staff on the paper have refused to work for the new editor appointed by Lukashenka. (IPI)

President Lukashenka threatened to withdraw the accreditation of journalists who covered a demonstration against the Belarus-Russia integration treaty, held on 2 April. He said that 'active negotiations' were already under way with Russian television channels and the journalists concerned 'will not be working here many days longer'. (SWB)

The Confederation of Journalists' Unions sent an open letter to President Lukashenka protesting at infringements of journalists' rights, and especially the sacking of media heads 'in contravention of judicial norms and charters of editorial boards'. The letter called on Lukashenka to hold a meeting with media representatives, to improve relations between the government and the press. (SWB)

Printing of the third volume of the official *Encyclopedia of Belarusian History* has been halted, it was revealed at a conference of historians in Stuttgart, Germany, on 12 April. The volume is reportedly to be purged of all material which takes a 'negative' attitude to the USSR, Communism and even Tsarist Russian rule. Belarusian historians are considering a

boycott of all future volumes of the *Encyclopedia*.

BOLIVIA

On 19 March **Osvald Calle**, a financial reporter with the daily *Ultima Hora*, received a death threat from an anonymous caller who told the paper: 'Tell him to stop investigating or we'll do away with him.' Calle has recently been covering the privatisation of state enterprises. (RSF)

A fight broke out between journalists with the **ERBOL press agency** and members of the National Revolutionary Movement (MNR, the senior party in the coalition government) on 8 April. The MNR members were trying to put posters on the front of the building in which ERBOL is based. (RSF)

BOSNIA-HERCEGOVINA

On 24 March **Ninko Djuric**, a journalist with the Pale-based weekly *Javnost*, was released from Tuzla district prison. He had been arrested by Bosnian police on 11 September 1995. According to the Bosnian Serb news agency, the fate of **Pedrag Popovici**, a journalist arrested with him, is still unknown. On 25 March **Hidajet Delic** (*Index* 2/1996), a Bosnian government news agency photographer also working for Associated Press, was freed by Bosnian Serb forces, apparently in exchange for Djuric. He had been detained in Pale for seven weeks, for three of which he was kept in a windowless freight container. (*Guardian*, CPJ, SWB)

On 29 March **Srecko Latal** of Associated Press was detained for several hours by Bosnian Serb police in Sarajevo near the border between Bosnian Federation and Serb zones. Latal had been assaulted by Serb youths before being taken by Bosnian Serb police operating inside Bosnian Federation territory. An IFOR patrol had attempted to rescue Latal but reportedly then handed him back to the Bosnian Serb police. He was later exchanged for two Serbs arrested earlier by Bosnian Federation police. Another journalist at the scene accused an IFOR soldier of threatening him with a gun when he attempted to intervene. (RSF, Reuter)

BOTSWANA

On 12 February vice-president Festus Mogae announced the introduction of a 10 per cent sales tax on privately owned newspaper sales, effective from 1 March. Journalists have expressed concern over the impact of the tax on the already falling circulation of newspapers within the country. (MISA)

A journalist from the privately owned *Botswana Guardian*, **Professor Malema**, has been threatened with prosecution if he refuses to reveal his sources for an article about a murder investigation. If found guilty of the charges, Malema could face up to 25 years in jail. (MISA)

BRAZIL

Diolinda Alves de Souza, a member of the Brazilian Landless Rural Workers

Movement, has been detained since 25 January in Alvares Machado, São Paulo, on charges of 'forming a criminal band'. The Movement is a legal organisation which campaigns for agrarian reform and has staged a number of land occupations. (AI)

The Ministry of Communication has ordered the closure of more than 300 community radio stations and the confiscation of their equipment, it was reported at the end of March. The measure was announced during negotiations between the Ministry and the Forum for the Democratisation of Communication, which is trying to establish a legal basis for community radio stations. (AMARC)

In recent months members of the **Casa da Paz** (Peace House), where 21 people were killed by the military police on 29 August 1993, have continued to be threatened and harassed by police (*Index* 1/1996). After the 1993 massacre, the Casa da Paz was converted into a community, education and legal advice centre used by relatives of the victims to lobby for compensation and justice. (AI)

Two journalists in the town of Smolyan were arrested and charged with defaming a public official on 20 February. **Dimitar Shtirkov** and **Valentin Hadzhiev**, of *Trud* and *24 Chasa* respectively, had both written articles alleging that the new district prosecutor in Devin had been dismissed

from the Smolyan police force in 1992 for corruption. They were released the following day. (OMRI, AI)

On 3 April prosecutor-general Ivan Tatarchev threatened to prosecute **Patriarch Maksim** in connection with the occupation by members of the Holy Synod of a candle factory owned by the schismatic 'alternative synod' of Metropolit Pimen. Bodyguards hired by Maksim occupied the factory in Sofia, claiming it is run illegally by rebel priests who do not recognise the Patriarch's authority. Pimen split from the official church in 1989, accusing Maksim and other top clergy of being stooges of the old regime. (OMRI, Reuter)

On 18 March **Par Par Lay, Lu Zaw, U Htway** and **U Aung Soe** were each sentenced to seven years in prison under the 1950 Emergency Provisions Act. Par Par Lay, Lu Zaw and U Htway were sentenced for performing at an Independence Day celebration at the home of NLD leader Aung San Suu Kyi (*Index* 2/1996). Nine other performers were arrested between January 7 and 10 but released without charge in early February. U Aung Soe was imprisoned in connection with the distribution of videos and speeches by Aung San Suu Kyi. (HRW)

Imprisoned journalists **Win Tin** and **Myo Myint Nyein** (*Index* 2/1996) were given additional sentences of five and seven years respectively on 28

March, for smuggling letters to Yozo Yokota, the UN special rapporteur for Burma. The letters detailed poor prison conditions and ill-treatment of inmates. (RSF)

Recent publication: *Kayin (Karen) State — The Killings Continue* (AI, April 1996, 17pp)

Lai Chandra, publisher of the newspaper *Vietnam Tudo* (Free Vietnam), was arrested and deported to Vietnam on 9 March. Officials said that he had been deported because of his alleged involvement with dissident Vietnamese trying to overthrow the Hanoi government. (SWB, *Far Eastern Economic Review*)

On 10 February *The Remains of a Ghost*, a television series made in Thailand, was banned for representing a Khmer cultural symbol as a blood-sucking ghost. (*Bangkok Post*)

The government has blocked plans for the US book retail chain Borders Inc to expand into Canada in order to protect one of Canada's 'cultural industries'. The decision, which was prompted by protests from Canadian booksellers and publishers, is permitted under the provisions of the North Atlantic Free Trade Agreement (NAFTA), in which US investors must obtain federal permits before they can buy or invest in cultural sectors such as broadcasting, publishing and bookselling. (*Financial Times*)

CHILE

The Santiago Court of Appeal issued a blanket prohibition order (under the 'abuse of publicity' law) on 16 April, preventing coverage by the Chilean media of a judicial investigation of the 1991 murder of senator **Jaime Guzmán Erraruriz**. (IAPA)

Recent publication: *Transition at the Crossroads — Human Rights Violations under Pinochet Remain the Crux* (AI, March 1996, 82pp)

CHINA

American films *GoldenEye* and *Apollo 13* were rejected by the censors in mid-February, the former because it 'focuses too directly on a foreign country'. The Oscar-winning *Babe* was also reportedly banned in early April. The prohibitions come amid fears of the negative impact of foreign imports on the Chinese film industry and the recent replacement of top government film official Tian Congming and the resignation of his associate, film importer Wu Mengchen, both of whom were responsible for bringing Hollywood blockbusters into China last year. In April it was reported that the Radio, Film and Television Ministry had ordered film director **Feng Xiaogang** to halt shooting on his new film *Relations Between Man and Woman* because it 'intentionally exaggerates dirty relations between men and women' and 'takes delight in showing ugliness instead of castigating ugliness'. Feng's most recent film, *Daddy*, has since been banned from public view by the Ministry, along

with his television drama *Love Dies Young. Steel is Made this Way*, by Lu Xuechang, and *Rice*, by **Huang Jianzhong**, have also been banned for being pornographic and depicting drug addiction. (*Variety*, Reuter)

Officials in Zhejiang province announced in early March that they will tear down tombs, temples and churches built without government approval, in an environmental and religious crackdown. The structures, often occupying valuable arable land, contravene recent state legislation ordering all places of worship to register with the government. (Reuter)

Five foreign journalists were expelled from Fujian province, the staging ground for recent missile tests in the Taiwan Straits, for allegedly gathering military secrets and violating State Security Law. **Shui An-teh** and **Chuang Chi-wei**, reporters for **Taiwan Television Enterprise**, were detained for two days and expelled on 9 March, for videoing troop exercises. Three Hong Kong reporters were detained on 10 March and expelled two days later. (CPJ, SWB, Reuter)

Chinese-American author **Amy Tan** was prevented from speaking at a banquet in aid of Chinese orphans at Beijing's Holiday Inn Lido on 31 March. Plainclothes security men, who originally hoped to ban the 'unauthorised' event altogether, raided the ballroom an hour before the evening was due to start, ripped down banners, partitioned the room

into three sections, and sent the chorus of children, gathered to greet the 450 guests, home early. (*Times*, Reuter, *International Herald Tribune*)

Xu Wenli (*Index* 2/1990), a prominent Democracy Wall activist, had his 15-year prison sentence formally revoked on 8 April. He continues to be deprived of his political rights until May 1997, however, and has been barred from meeting foreigners and publishing his writings. (Reuter)

China is to crack down on pirated, pornographic, or politically suspect television programmes, often shown by poor regional stations in an effort to boost ratings and raise advertising revenue, Xinhua news agency reported in mid-April. Last year eight stations were fined and suspended for cutting official Chinese Television programming and advertising in favour of smuggled, pornographic or otherwise taboo shows. (*South China Morning Post*)

Inner Mongolia: Ten people detained in mid-December 1995 are still being held, accused of organising a pro-democracy group. They include **Hada**, **Hei Long** and **Shuangzhu**, detained in Hohot on 10 December; **Tegexi**, **Chen Haishan**, **Chang Ming**, **Dogtengbayar**, and **Bao Qingshan**, detained on 11 and 12 December. Detainees' houses were also searched and documents and addresses relating to national autonomy were removed from Hada's home. Twenty-six students who protested against

SALLY OLDING

the detentions on 16 and 30 December were themselves detained briefly and three — **Xinjiltu, Gabiyatu,** and **Hasibagen** — are believed to remain in detention. Hada's wife, **Xinna,** was arrested and charged with inciting the demonstrations on 16 December and released on 12 January. She has since been rearrested, apparently for giving an interview to **Voice of America** radio and informing 'foreign reactionary organisations' about the events. (Reuter, AI, SWB)

Recent publications: *Gross Human Rights Violations Continue* (AI, February 1996, 22pp); *State Secrets — A Pretext for Repression* (AI, March 1996, 9pp)

CROATIA

In March lawyers representing 15 people charged with spying for Croatian Serb rebels and the rump Yugoslavia accused military prosecutors of preventing them from mounting a defence by denying them access to necessary legal documents. They also complained that the prisoners were brought to the court in chains. (OMRI)

On 29 March Parliament passed a Penal Code amendment relating to libel against the state's highest officials — the president, prime minister, the presidents of both houses of Parliament and of the Constitutional and Supreme Courts — whereby proceedings can be initiated by the state prosecutor and not the offended party. Another amendment passed the same day creates a new offence of disclosure and publication of state secrets at a time when, according to the Croatian Journalists' Association, almost any piece of information can be described as a state secret. The new laws will re-establish the 'crimes of the media' law abolished in 1991 if signed into law by President Tudjman. Penalties would range from six months to three years in prison. (RSF, SWB, CPJ, Reuter)

CUBA

On 23 February **Lázaro González Valdes** and **Leonel Morejón Almagro,** leaders of the non-governmental coalition group **Concilio Cubano** (*Index* 2/1996), were sentenced to 14 months and 15 months in prison respectively for 'disobedience' and 'disrespect', apparently for having ignored police warnings to cease their political activities. **René Gómez Manzano,** a founder of Concilio Cubano and president of the unofficial lawyers group Agramontist Current, **Reinaldo Cosano Alén** and **Mercedes Parada Antúnez**, both deputy national organisers of the group, are also in detention following their arrest in February. The crackdown on Concilio Cubano, in which dozens of activists were rounded up and held for periods from several hours to several days, prevented the organisation from holding its first national convention, which had been planned for 24 February. (AI)

Rafael Solano, director of the independent news agency **Habana Press**, was freed on 8 April, after being detained since 27 February. He has been charged with 'association with persons with the intent to commit a crime', an offence which carries a maximum three-year sentence. **Roxana Valdivia** (*Index* 2/1996), a journalist with **Independent Cuban Press Bureau (BPIC)**, reported in early March that she was told she must emigrate or else face charges of refusing to obey orders to cease her work as an independent journalist. On 20 March she was granted a visa to leave Cuba for the US. On 13 April the Communist Party weekly *Granma International* accused independent journalists of being 'instruments trying to destroy Cuba's social and political gains and snatch away the island's independence'. The government, it said, has every right to take 'any actions necessary to defend and guarantee its national sovereignty'. The article also accused international free speech groups of 'orchestrating a worldwide campaign...to

accuse Cuba of persecution and massive detentions of journalists'. (CPJ, RSF, Associated Press)

DENMARK

The neo-Nazi **Danish National Socialist Movement (DNSB)** inaugurated its new station, **Radio Oasis**, on 28 February (*Index* 5/1995). The Community Broadcasting Committee finally granted the station a licence to broadcast twice weekly, subject to rules against inciting racial hatred. The DNSB advocates forcible deportation of Denmark's Jewish community to Israel. Radio Oasis presently broadcasts on a weak 30-watt transmitter, shared with other community broadcasters, but has already applied for access to a cable radio network, which would give it a much bigger audience in the whole of Roskilde county, south of Copenhagen. DNSB chairman Jonni Hansen admits that if his party were ever to attain political power it would end the tolerance that allows his group to broadcast. 'We would limit others' freedom of speech,' he said. (Reuter, *Berlingske Tidende*)

EGYPT

Mahmoud al-Maraghy, editor-in-chief of weekly *al-Arabi*, and **Gamal Fahmi**, an *al-Arabi* columnist, were sentenced to six months' imprisonment on 4 April for 'slandering a member of Parliament'. The charges resulted from an editorial denouncing an article written by Tharwat Abadha which criticised former president

Gamal Abdel Nasser. (RSF)

Recent publications: *Democracy Jeopardized: Nobody 'Passed' the Elections* (Egyptian Organisation for Human Rights, February 1996, 163pp); *Recurrent Detention — Prisoners Without Trial* (EOHR, February 1996, 274pp)

ETHIOPIA

Terefe Mengesha, former editor-in-chief of the Amharic weekly *Roha*, was sentenced to one year in prison in February, shortly after completing a one-year sentence for 'publishing false information' and 'inciting the public to anxiety and insecurity'. (CPJ)

Arrests and intimidation of suspected **Oromo Liberation Front** supporters have intensified since mid-February. The detainees are being held without charge and have not been allowed access to legal representation or their families. There are particular fears for the safety of **Teshome Mutama**, whose whereabouts since his disappearance are not known and there have been reports of the death of another, **Challa Kebebe**, as a result of torture. (AI, AAASHRAN)

Soloman Lemma, editor of the independent Amharic-language weekly *Wolafen* was sentenced to 18 months in prison on 7 March for publishing 'false reports to incite war and unrest'. (CPJ)

Iskinder Nega, editor-in-chief of the popular independent English-language weekly *Habesha*, was charged with 'writing derogatory statements against the government and government officials' on 26 March. The charge apparently arose from a cartoon depicting someone whom officials interpreted as prime minister Meles Zanawi falling under the foot of US president Bill Clinton. Nega was initially abducted from his home on 1 March and held incommunicado until being charged. Nega had been due to launch a new Amharic-language newspaper on 6 March. And on 25 March **Tesfaye Tegen**, editor-in-chief of the Amharic weekly *Beza*, was jailed in connection with a cartoon published in late 1995 depicting Meles and government officials as members of a football team. (CPJ)

Six editors, reporters and clerical employees of the newspapers *Ethiop* and *Tekwami* were detained on 26 March as the papers were being printed in the city of Bole. All were released by 5 April, but neither paper was printed during that week. (CPJ)

A meeting was held by the president of the Central High Court on 12 April to consider the scope of reporting restrictions on the genocide trials. Originally, restrictions had been imposed to prevent verbatim reports of prosecution witnesses' testimony which, it was believed, might affect the testimony of other witnesses. According to the latest ruling, journalists may report the proceedings, without identifying witnesses, at the end of every case. The trial itself was again adjourned on 11 April, the sixth adjournment since it began in December 1994. Seventy-one former Dergue officials are charged with genocide and crimes against humanity. Forty-six have pleaded not guilty; the other 25, including former President Mengistu, are being tried in absentia. (Reuter, *Independent*, SWB)

EUROPEAN UNION

The Justice and Internal Affairs Council secured agreement on a common EU plan for joint action against racism and xenophobia on 19 March. Member states pledged to take steps to combat, among other things, public incitement to discrimination, violence or racial hatred; public apology with a racist or xenophobic goal for crimes against humanity or human rights violations; the dissemination or public distribution of racist or xenophobic writings or pictures; participation in activities of groups that involve racial, ethnic or religious hatred. The United Kingdom had argued from the start that the agreement should take the form of a non-binding resolution. In the end, the UK reserved the right not to criminalise certain forms of speech, such as publicly denying the Holocaust. (Agence Europe)

Recent publication: *Concerns in Europe July-December 1995* (AI, March 1996, 64pp)

FRANCE

The Council of Europe has ordered France to pay compensation to three people whose telephones were tapped in a judicial inquiry in the 1980s. A book published in January, *The Ears of the President*, has alleged that telephone tapping has long been used illegally in French politics, particularly during President Mitterrand's first seven years in office. The book's authors, Jean-Marie Pontaut and Jerome Dupuis, claim that between 1983 and 1986 the government tapped the phone lines of 2,000 people, 128 of whom were journalists. (Reuter)

GAMBIA

Chikeluba Kenechuku, a journalist for the *Daily Observer*, was forcibly deported to Senegal on 16 April. Kenechuku, a Nigerian citizen, has been routinely harassed by Gambian security forces since late last year. In March this year he fled to Senegal after receiving threats from Gambian security agents over his work with the *Daily Observer*. On his return to Gambia on 30 March he was arrested, interrogated, beaten and held incommunicado. (CPJ)

GREECE

In February parliamentary president Apostolos Kaklamanis accused television stations **Mega**, **Antenna** and **Star** of disseminating Turkish propaganda in their coverage of Turkish soldiers planting their flag on the disputed islet of Imia/Kardak (*Index* 2/1996). On 14 February the National Audio-Visual

Council said that the coverage lacked 'journalistic ethics'. The opposition has accused the government of attempting to gag the media to conceal its mistaken handling of the crisis. (OMRI)

GUATEMALA

On 12 February **Débora Guzmán Chupén**, a trade unionist at the Lunafil clothing factory, received an anonymous letter threatening her with death. Both she and her husband **Félix González**, a Lunafil union leader, have since received numerous death threats, despite moving to a secret location. Guzmán was kidnapped in February 1995 and warned that she would be killed if her husband did not cease his union activities. (AI)

On 14 February forensic experts began exhuming a mass grave under a children's playground in Rabinal containing the remains of 22 to 100 Achi indians massacred in the early 1980s. The army had a base on the site before converting it into a playground in 1982. The same forensic team has already completed three other exhumations in Rabinal. Church sources claim that 19 separate massacres were carried out in Rabinal in the early 1980s. Another forensic investigation at Agua Fria, Quiché province, discovered the charred remains of 167 Quiché-Maya men, women and children on 27 February. So far 11 mass graves have been unearthed in the area, but experts believe that hundreds more remain. (Reuter)

Marco Vinicio Pacheco, a journalist with **Radio Sonora**, was kidnapped and tortured by four armed men while on his way to the Assembly of the Social Communication Workers Unions of Guatemala on 28 February. After his release from hospital Pacheco went into hiding but the threats against him continued. He left the country with UN assistance on 19 March. (FIP)

On 27 February **Vilma Cristina González** was abducted, tortured and raped by armed men in civilian clothes, who warned her that she and her brother would be killed if they do not leave the country. Her brother, **Reynaldo Federico González**, is secretary-general of the Federation of Trade Unions of Bank and Insurance Employees of Guatemala and, on 20 January, was appointed as one of the main spokesmen of the Gran Alianza Sindical, an umbrella organisation comprising 11 trade unions. (AI)

Congress ratified the International Labour Organisation convention on indigenous rights on 5 March. The convention covers many issues, including the right of indigenous people to live on ancestral lands. Mayan peasants are currently occupying a dozen large farms demanding the return of ancestral lands to which they hold land registry documents but which, they say, were stolen earlier this century. More than 20 leaders were jailed during recent government efforts to reoccupy two estates in the province of San Marcos but a judge ordered their release after 400 angry protesters descended on the police station. (Reuter, *Mesoamerica*)

At the end of March **Juan José Yantuche**, a journalist with the programme *TV Noticias*, was discovered in a coma in his car in the city of Mixco. He had gunshot wounds to his chest and abdomen. He died in hospital on 11 April. Police have not yet opened any investigation into his death. (RSF)

A group of men broke into the home of *Ultima Hora* journalist **Erwin San Juan** on 9 April. The men searched the house, stole money and equipment and told San Juan 'if you continue reporting, the next time will be your last.' (FIP)

Recent publication: *Summary of Amnesty International's Concerns, January 1995-January 1996* (AI, 1996, 10pp)

GUINEA

On 13 March **Souleymane Diallo**, managing director of the newspaper *Le Lynx*, was arrested and accused of 'falsification of documents' under Article 75 of the Press Law. He faces up to five years in prison and a fine of US$2,000 if convicted. (RSF)

HAITI

In early March police in Port-au-Prince threatened **Liliane Pierre Paul**, co-director of **Radio Kiskeya**, and **François Rotchild**, a reporter with **Radio Metropole**, after they broadcast protests made by human rights groups against police tactics during a 7 March confrontation between police and a group called 'Red Army', which led to the deaths of seven people. (RSF)

Recent publication: *A Question of Justice* (AI, 1996, 20pp)

HONDURAS

The Supreme Court ruled unanimously on 18 January that the 1991 amnesty laws are unconstitutional, opening the way for military officers accused of kidnapping and torture of students in the 1980s to stand trial in a civilian court for the first time (*Index* 2/1996). Seven officers are in custody, and warrants have been issued for the arrest of three officers in hiding. (*Mesoamerica, Latinamerica Press*)

Recent publication: *Continued Struggle Against Impunity* (AI, March 1996, 21pp)

HONG KONG

Vietnamese dissident writer and activist **Nguyen Thi Thoi** was forcibly repatriated on 12 March. Thoi, who fled Vietnam in 1989, has been sentenced in absentia to five years in prison for anti-government activities abroad. (PEN)

The Beijing-appointed Preparatory Committee voted to scrap Hong Kong's elected legislature on 24 March. The Xinhua news agency announced on 25 March that Democratic Party members will be ineligible to sit on the provisional legislative council which replaces it. Civil servants were told on 26 March that they must pledge undivided allegiance to the provisional legislature or lose their jobs. (*Guardian, Independent, Financial Times*)

Three films were withdrawn from the Hong Kong Film Festival, which opened on 26 March. The films — *Warrior Lanling, the King of Masks* and *The Story of Wang Laobai* — were removed by their copyright owners, apparently under pressure from the mainland. The China Film Bureau consistently refuses to send unauthorised films to the Festival. (*South China Morning Post*, Reuter)

Protesters clashed with police as they met to commemorate the 20th anniversary of China's pro-democracy April Fifth Movement. One demonstrator was injured when police tried to prevent the group from placing a wreath in front of the main entrance to the Xinhua news agency. (Reuter)

INDIA

Novelist **Salman Rushdie** petitioned the Supreme Court at the beginning of February to overrule the decision by the Customs Department to bar his book *The Moor's Last Sigh* from the country. The objection to the book seems to be that a dog is named after Jawaharlal Nehru, independent India's first prime minister. On 9 April the Delhi High Court ruled that the Customs Department must state their reasons for the ban within three weeks. (Reuter, *Times*)

The body of **Jalil Andrabi**, chairman of the Kashmir Commission of Jurists, was pulled from the Jhelum River at Srinagar on 27 March. Andrabi had been due to attend the UN Human Rights Commission (UNHRC) meeting in Geneva. Anrabi's widow claimed the Indian army killed him while he was in their custody. He had been abducted on 9 March. (AI, Reuter)

The body of **Ghulam Rasool Sheikh**, editor of *Rehnuma-e-Kashmir* and *Saffron Times*, was found in the Jhelum River on 10 April. He had been abducted by militants, believed to be backed by the Indian authorities, on 28 March. On 11 April, Abdul Gani Lone and Syed Ali Shah Geelani, both prominent Kashmiri separatist leaders, accused the Indian government of setting up death squads to eliminate opponents before the May parliamentary elections. Both men have survived recent assassination attempts. (Reuter)

Recent publications: *Amnesty International and India* (AI, March 1996, 43pp); *Communal Violence and the Denial of Justice* (HRW/Asia, April 1996, 30pp)

INDONESIA

The Indonesian government banned all news-stand sales of the March issue of *Reader's Digest* magazine. The ban eliminated 10,000 copies from news-stand circulation; 2,300 subscriber copies delivered by post were not affected. It appears the ban came in reaction to a profile in the March issue of East Timorese human rights advocate Bishop Carlos Belo, which included detailed allegations of human rights abuses by Indonesian authorities in East Timor. (Committee to Protect Journalists, *Jakarta Post*)

The Indonesian Ulema Council (MUI) have begun a campaign to prevent the screening of the Hollywood film *Executive Decision*. The MUI succeeded in having the film *Schindler's List* banned in 1994 and last year forced the withdrawal of the film *True Lies* after one week. The Committee of Islamic Solidarity is also seeking to ban the film, for misleading the international public 'by characterising Muslims as a bunch of terrorists.' (*Jakarta Post*)

Recent publication: *Indonesia and East Timor — When Will the Commission Take Action?* (AI, February 1996, 38pp)

IRAN

Abbas Maroufi, editor of *Gardoun* magazine, was sentenced to 35 lashes and six months in prison for publishing lies, insulting the former leader of the Islamic Republic of Iran and for publishing immoral poems on 29 January. Maroufi is also barred from journalism for two years. (AI)

Ahmad Masjed Jame'i, the deputy minister of cultural and Islamic guidance, resigned in February in protest at new censorship guidelines introduced in time for the Majlis elections on 8 March. The new guidelines followed

soon after accusations made by the Islamic guidance minister that the press did not understand its proper limits. (*Iran Times*, HRW, SWB)

The daily paper *Salam* was suspended for two days on 7 March, apparently for violating electoral law by planning to publish a front-page story predicting electoral defeat for the government in the Majlis elections. According to a Human Rights Watch report, the elections themselves took place under severely restricted conditions: around 44 per cent of prospective candidates were barred from standing by the Council of Guardians; opposition gatherings were frequently attacked by pro-government mobs; a press conference held by the Liberation Party of Iran was broken up by armed Interior Ministry troops, who confiscated foreign correspondents' video footage of the event; and the weekly paper *Bahar* was suspended indefinitely by the Islamic Guidance Ministry the week before the vote, without any reason given. (RSF, HRW, *Independent*)

Recent publication: *Power versus Choice — Human Rights and Parliamentary Elections in the Islamic Republic of Iran* (HRW/Middle East, March 1996, 19pp)

ISRAEL

Palestinian journalists have been prevented from travelling to and from Gaza and the West Bank by travel blockades imposed by Israeli security forces since 13 February,

following Hamas bus bombings in Israel that have killed 58 people. The restrictions are severely hampering their ability to cover the situation in Israel from a Palestinian perspective. On 3 March **Hisham Abdallah**, a journalist with **Agence France-Presse**, was detained by Israeli police while on his way to his office in Jerusalem. (IFJ)

Over 200 students from Bir Zeit University, near Ramallah in the West Bank, were arrested after security forces raided university premises and surrounding areas on 28 March as part of the crackdown on Hamas members and supporters. The raids were also intended to round up students from Gaza, currently banned from travelling to the West Bank. Security forces reportedly put stickers saying 'Shipped to Gaza' on the backs of 32 Gazan students who were deported. (*Jerusalem Times*, Bir Zeit University)

Sha'wan Rateb Jabarin, a fieldworker for human rights organisation **al-Haq**, is still detained without charge in Atlit Prison. He was arrested under an administrative detention order on 5 February. (Arab Association for Human Rights)

ITALY

The Italian state broadcaster RAI has refused to show advertisements for *I Dance Alone*, a film by **Bernardo Bertolucci**, whose *Last Tango in Paris* was banned in Italy 20 years ago, has called the RAI decision absurd, as

RAI had not even seen the film before the ban. After *Last Tango in Paris*, Bertolucci was given a two-month suspended prison sentence and deprived of the right to vote for five years. (*Times*)

JAPAN

New Zealand author **James Mackay** received a death threat from an anonymous man in mid-February, in an apparent attempt to prevent publication of his forthcoming book on Japanese war crimes. Having refused large bribes to scrap the book late last year, Mackay was told in a phone call that 'there are other ways of persuading you'. (Jiji Press Newswire)

Curators of a revised exhibition in Nagasaki's Atomic Bomb Museum bowed to right-wing pressure in March and removed controversial photographs and text from display. The material — introduced to deflect criticism that the exhibition had ignored Japan's war atrocities — drew complaints from local dignitaries and a formal protest from conservative members of the city assembly. Items depicting the Rape of Nanking and the Bataan Death March have been replaced by pictures of victorious Japanese soldiers and the attack on Pearl Harbor. (*Independent*)

JORDAN

Laith Shubeilat, an outspoken trade unionist and political commentator, was sentenced by a military court to three years' imprisonment on 17 March for slandering King Hussein and Queen Noor. He has regularly spoken out against the Israeli-Palestinian agreements, called for a constitutional monarchy in Jordan, and condemned Queen Noor for weeping at Israeli prime minister Rabin's funeral. Shubeilat plans to appeal. (*Independent*)

Salameh Ne'mat (*Index* 6/1995), Jordan correspondent for the London-based paper *al-Hayat*, and his editor **Jihad al-Khazen** (*Index* 2/1996, p50) were cleared of the defamation charges against them on 20 April.

KAZAKHSTAN

Itar-Tass reported in early April that several Slavic groups, including the **Lad (Harmony)** movement and the **Slavic Culture Society**, have been banned for six months for holding rallies in support of the Russian State Duma's decision of 15 March to annul the 1991 Belovezhskaya Pushcha accords which abolished the Soviet Union. (SWB)

According to a report released by the Kazakhstan-American Bureau on Human Rights on 9 April, independent journalists are increasingly being persecuted by the state, often by means of defamation charges. The reports also claimed that a new censorship system has been introduced by the State Radio and Television Committee. (OMRI)

KENYA

On 26 February two men appealing against a 10-year sentence for robbery with violence were sentenced to death after the High Court in Nakuru ruled that this was the sentence they should initially have received. This remarkable precedent could have extremely grave consequences in a number of cases, with defendants sentenced to terms of imprisonment choosing not to appeal for fear of receiving a capital sentence. Koigi wa Wamwere and his two fellow accused (*Index* 2/1995, 6/1995, 2/1996), charged with attempted robbery and sentenced to four years' imprisonment, are currently awaiting to launch an appeal. (AI)

Parliamentarian **Kipruto arap Kirwa** of the ruling KANU party disappeared a few days after holding a press conference on 28 March at which he openly criticised President Moi for his failure to tolerate criticism. There are serious concerns for his safety. (MISA)

KYRGYZSTAN

The **Ittipak Society of Ethnic Uighurs** was banned for three months by order of the Justice Ministry in early April for 'separatist' activities. A Kyrgyz radio report said the Ittipak Society was carrying out 'a policy contradicting the interests of the Chinese people' and was violating the Kyrgyz-China communiqué of 1992, on non-interference in internal affairs. (SWB)

President Akayev dismissed the editors of two leading newspapers — *Slovo*

Kyrgyzstana and *Svobodnye Gory* — and the head of the State Television and Radio Committee in early April. Authorities said the move was consistent with state policy of rotating 'cadres of the state-owned mass media'. The papers are jointly owned by their employees and the state. Editorial staff at both papers signed an open letter in protest at the dismissals. The letter was due to be published in the 10 April edition of *Slovo Kyrgyzstana*, but the edition was reportedly prevented from going to press by the Presidential Office. (OMRI, SWB)

MALAYSIA

The deputy prime minister Anwar Ibrahim said on 7 March that the government has no plans to censor the Internet. At the launch of the Internet World '96 conference he said: 'Simply closing our doors will not only hurt us but will push us back in the race for growth and prosperity.' , On 3 April, however, the prime minister, Mahathir Mohamad, called for international action to stop 'dirty literature from flowing to other nations' over the Internet. (Reuter, *Business Times*)

Irene Fernandez, director of Tenaganita, a women's rights organisation in Kuala Lumpur, was arrested and charged with 'false reporting' on 18 March. The charge arose fromTenaganita's investigation into abuses against migrant workers in Malaysia's immigration detention centres. If convicted, Fernandez faces a

maximum possible sentence of three years in prison. (HRW)

The authorities initially refused to issue a visa to the Yugoslav delegate to the International Association of Sports Press (AIPS) congress, held in Kuala Lumpur from 25-30 March. AIPS president Togay Bayatli of Turkey intervened personally with the organisers for visas to be issued to the delegates of Yugoslavia and Israel, another country on the blacklist. (SWB)

Opposition leader Tunku Razaleigh Hamzah has reached a six-figure out-of-court settlement with the British daily *Independent* over a 1994 allegation that the former finance minister had illegally received 25 million shares from Hong Kong-based property firm Carrian. The newspaper also made a formal apology. (*Far Eastern Economic Review*)

MALI

On 22 February **Tiengoum Boubeye Maiga** and **Aboubacar Saliph Diarra**, publishing director and editor-in-chief respectively of the pro-government paper *Les Echos,* were convicted of defaming Oumar Mariko, secretary-general of the Malian Students' Association. The charge arose from an article published on 15 August 1995, questioning the use of funds that Mariko had received from a German humanitarian organisation. Maiga and Diarra were jailed for one month and ordered to pay damages of CFA one million (US$1,970) each. (CPJ)

MAURITANIA

The independent weekly magazine *Mauritanie-Nouvelles* was banned by the interior ministry for three months from 11 April. The action comes after four earlier suspensions, two in March: the 17 March edition was seized under Article 11 of the press law following publication of a story about the status of women, and the 25 March edition for running a story on slavery, a practice that the government claims has been eradicated. **Bah Ould Saleck**, the magazine's editor, resigned on 28 March in protest at the continuing harassment of the magazine by the government and intends to lodge an appeal against the government for misuse of power. (SWB, Reuter)

MEXICO

Following the break-up by security forces of a peaceful demonstration by indigenous people demanding an end to oil spills and compensation for pollution in Tabasco, 107 people, including **Rafael López Cruz**, president of the state committee of the opposition Democratic Revolutionary Party (PRD), and other PRD members and peasants are being held in incommunicado detention. Many of them are believed to be charged with sabotage, sedition and criminal association. (AI)

Angel Valdovinos Garza, a member of the **Southern Sierra Peasant Organisation** (OCSS), has disappeared after being seen driven away from a bus station in Acapulco by Guerrero state officials on 26 January. **Valdovinos** had earlier been threatened for his work on behalf of 40 families who face eviction from Las Antenas where a new tourist resort is planned. He is the second senior OCSS member to have disappeared within a year. On 7 February OCSS leader **Rocío Mesino Mesino** was followed in Acapulco, Guerrero, by three men in a car who tried to kidnap her. The OCSS has publicly denounced the role of the state in the Guerrero massacre of 1995. **Paula Galeana Balanzar**, whose husband was killed in the massacre, was visited at home on 8 February by three men claiming to be from the State Office for Internal Affairs. They took photographs and told **Galeana** that she would regret her actions in seeking compensation. On 6 March members of peasant communities in Guerrero began a mass hunger strike to protest the closing of the case and exoneration of local authorities. (AI, *Latinamerica Press*)

On 28 February **José Barrón Rosales**, a journalist with **Radio Huayacocotla** in the state of Veracruz, was shot at and verbally abused. Rosales was not harmed but continues to receive threats. His assailant, although identified to the authorities, has not been arrested. (AI)

Recent publication: *Overcoming Fear — Human Rights Violations Against Women in Mexico* (AI, March 1996, 29pp)

NETHERLANDS

Parliament voted in favour of a motion on 16 April to grant homosexual partners all the legal rights and duties of married couples. The government, however, has shown some reluctance to enact the motion into law. It has promised to review the situation and report on its legislative plans 'in several weeks'. Although gay couples have for some time been legally entitled to register their relationships as 'partnership contracts', the new parliamentary proposal would give them the same status as married couples in terms of property inheritance, pensions and rights over any children from previous relationships. (*Times*)

NIGERIA

A National Theatre production of **Wole Soyinka**'s play *The Trial of Brother Jero* due to begin on 27 February was reportedly stopped from going ahead by members of the State Security Service. (*ThisDay*)

In early March **Jude Sinee**, a newspaper vendor in the Ogoni settlement of Bori, was arrested by armed agents of the Rivers State Internal Security Task Force who also confiscated 500 copies of various publications. No reason was given for his arrest, and Sinee is still in detention. (CPJ)

Recent publication: *A Summary of Human Rights Concerns* (AI, March 1996, 11pp)

PAKISTAN

On 26 February the government approved electoral reforms that will give non-Muslims the right to vote for general parliamentary seats as well as for seats reserved for their communities. Non-Muslims make up about three per cent of the total population. The proposed law will also abolish identity cards for voters. The Pakistan Muslim League, the main opposition party, rejected the reforms accusing the government of vote-rigging by giving non-Muslims what amounts to two votes. (Reuter)

The Human Rights Commission of Pakistan (HRCP) report for 1995, issued on 28 February, reports that over 2,000 people, including 40 children, were killed in Karachi during the year. At least 260 people died in police custody or in 'encounters' with the police. So far this year over 175 people have been killed in Karachi. (Reuter)

Recent publications: *Human Rights Crisis in Karachi* (AI, February 1996, 43pp); *State of Human Rights in 1995* (Human Rights Commission of Pakistan, February 1996, 244pp)

PALESTINE (AUTONOMOUS AREAS)

Palestinian police raided a student meeting at **An-Najah University** in Nablus, West Bank, on 30 March, firing live ammunition and setting off tear gas, which injured three people. The meeting had been called to protest mass arrests of suspected Hamas sympathisers. President Yasser Arafat visited the university on 5 April and apologised for the raid. (Reuter)

Recent publication: *Critique of the Press Law 1995 Issued by the Palestinian Authority: Series Study 1* (Palestinian Centre for Human Rights, 1995, 52pp)

PERU

Journalist **Jesus Alfonso Castiglione Mendoza**, who was sentenced to 20 years' imprisonment for membership of the Shining Path, is still waiting for his case to be reviewed (*Index* 1/1996). The 'faceless' court, which passed the sentence in November 1995, has yet to return the file to the Lima Superior Court, preventing any review of the case. **Castiglione** has been in detention since 29 April 1993. (Instituto Prensa y Sociedad)

SUNAT, the government agency responsible for policing taxation and contraband, has ceased advertising in the business daily **Gestión** in response to articles published in early March which criticised the agency and the government's economic adjustment programme. (Instituto Prensa y Sociedad)

PHILIPPINES

Four people were arrested for taking part in protest rallies against proposed anti-terrorism legislation in Cagayan de Oro City on 8 February. Conrado Kimura was briefly detained in the village of Lapasan and

accused of encouraging protesters to build barricades along the Lapasan highway. (*Philippine Human Rights Update*)

Herman Tiu Laurel, a journalist for the paper *Today*, was arrested on 15 March and accused by the Commission on Elections of 'falsification' in connection with his recent senatorial candidacy for the People's Reform Party. Laurel is well known for his criticism of the Commission chairman, Bernardo Pardo. (*Business World*)

Two journalists were shot at close range on the evening of 20 March in Cotabato City, Mindano, in the second attack on the press in six weeks. **Ali Macabalang**, a part-time reporter for Reuter, was shot in the leg and his companion, **Nash Maulana**, a correspondent for the *Philippine Daily Inquirer*, was hit in the leg by a gunman described as 'professional'. They have been placed under armed guard in hospital. (Reuter)

POLAND

More than 60 senators from different parties signed a letter to the Supreme Audit Chamber on 23 February, demanding an immediate audit of the state television company. They accused the company of financial mismanagement, incompetence, waste and inefficiency. The opposition Conservative Party reacted by accusing the ruling Democratic Left Alliance of trying to bring public

broadcasting under political control and of planning to force television chairman Wieslaw Walendziak to resign. (SWB)

ROMANIA

In late February the World Jewish Congress accused the Association of Swiss Bankers of hiding data on the fate of property belonging to Romanian Jews who were 'romanianised' during WWII. Details of a fortune allegedly amassed in an account at the Swiss Volksbank in the name of Radu Lecca have reportedly been discovered in Securitate files, according to which Lecca was refused access to the account in 1963 on the grounds that the bank's records had been destroyed. (OMRI)

On 29 February Senator Ticu Dumitrecu of the National Peasant Party-Christian Democratic announced a personal boycott of parliamentary debates in protest at the indefinite postponement of debate on a bill proposed two years ago providing for the release of information on the Securitate and allowing citizens access to their Securitate files. He also criticised Parliament's blocking of another proposed law aimed at banning former Communist officials from holding high public office within the administration. (OMRI)

On 4 March the Senate approved an amendment to the Penal Code penalising the use of foreign state symbols. Those who sing other states' national anthems or display the flag or other symbols of another state could be imprisoned for up to three years. The law has yet to be debated by the Chamber of Deputies. (SWB)

On 19 March both chambers of Parliament sitting in joint session passed a law allowing the setting up of political parties organised along ethnic lines. The law represents a compromise after previous versions had been criticised as infringing on the right to free association because they prevented the legal registration of political parties with fewer than 10,000 members in 21 of Romania's 40 counties. (OMRI, Reuter)

RUSSIAN FEDERATION

On 6 February **Alexander Nikitin** was arrested by agents of the Federal Security Service and accused of espionage in connection with his report for the Norwegian environmental group, Bellona, on radioactive contamination of Murmansk Oblast. Nikitin was charged under the 1993 Law on State Secrets, which specifically excludes information 'on the condition of the environment' from classification. Nikitin's application for bail was rejected on 9 April. (*International Herald Tribune*, OMRI)

On 20 February the Prosecutor's Office dropped all charges for financial irregularities against the satirical television puppet show *Kukly* (*Index* 5/1995). A spokesman said the irregularities were 'too insignificant' to bother with. (SWB)

Alexander Krutov, a correspondent for the daily *Moskovski Novosti* in the Volga region, was attacked by two men who beat him with metal pipes on 23 February. (CPJ)

Freelance photojournalist **Felix Solovyov** was shot dead by unidentified gunmen in central Moscow on 26 February. The motive for his murder is unclear and police have made no progress in finding his killers. (CPJ)

Communist Party leader Gennady Zyuganov accused the national media — especially television — of conducting an 'information blockade' against his presidential campaign, Itar-Tass reported on 9 April. *Ekho Moskvy* replied to the accusation by saying 'space costs money, there is more interesting material to publish, and there is a Communist press to build up Zyuganov's image.' (OMRI)

Former Soviet dissident **Valeriya Novodvorskaya** (*Index* 2/1988), currently head of the Democratic Union of Russia, has been charged with 'deliberate instigation of inter-ethnic enmity' by 'repeatedly expressing opinions and spreading ideas suggesting the inferiority of the Russian nation'. The charge arises from articles in *Novyi Vzglyad* and an interview with Estonian television, in which Novodvorskaya descrribed 'manic-depressive psychosis as an indispensable part of the Russian character'. (SWB)

Chechnya: Nadezhda

Chaikova, a reporter for the weekly *Obshchaya Gazeta* who went missing on 20 March while covering the Chechen conflict, was found dead near the village of Gekhi, southwest of Grozny, on 30 March. She had been severely beaten, forced to her knees and shot in the back of the head. Chaikova was well known for her hard-hitting coverage of the war, and for her exposé of the use of special 'filtration' camps by Russian authorities to control the population. (Reuter)

Mehmet Ali Tekin and **Talip Ozcevik**, journalists with the conservative Turkish daily *Selam*, were sentenced to three years in prison in early April for attempting to enter Chechnya from Azerbaijan, via Dagestan. Russia has repeatedly accused elements in Turkey of supporting the Chechen rebels. (OMRI)

RWANDA

Journalist **Joseph Runyezi** was arrested on 29 March by soldiers of the Rwandan Patriotic Army and charged with participating in 'secret meetings'. Runyezi , a Hutu, works for the Kinyarwanda-language programme of Radio Rwanda. Since being arrested Runyezi has disappeared. (RSF)

In a press conference on 9 April vice-president Paul Kagame castigated the media for exaggerating the refugee problem. He said that the government was ready to receive any influx of refugees and would provide the necessary arrangements for

Belgrade's culture wars

by Adem Demaci

Ethnic Albanians make up 90 per cent of the population in the Serbian enclave of Kosovo, but in every way they are second-class citizens

THE regime in Belgrade is systematically destroying our Albanian culture. First they took our radio and TV from us by abolishing the Albanian-language service, in July 1990. The following month they closed our daily paper, *Rilindja* (*Index* 8/1990). Not too long after that they took over the library of Kosova University. They burned all the books, journals, papers and publications in Albanian. In this way they destroyed our information system.

Then they closed the company Kosova-Film, the Institute for History, the State Archive of Kosova, the Institute for Statistics. Then they banned secondary and tertiary education for Albanians. (It was after that that the so-called 'parallel education system' began, the quality of which is extremely poor.)

They have taken over the Provincial Theatre, they have closed the Shota Ensemble, and many other cultural organisations. They have closed the Academy of Science and Arts of Kosova and the Albanological Institute in Prishtina.

Right now we have a daily paper, *Bujku*, which doesn't have a publishing permit, which is not allowed to have a bank account. It could be banned, or closed at any time.

Ethnic Albanian writer **Adem Demaci,** *president of the Committee for the Defence of Human rIghts and Freedoms in Kosovo, served a total of 28 years on charges of subversive activities and disseminating hostile propaganda before his release in April 1990. He was awarded the Andrei Sakharov Prize for Freedom of Speech in 1991*

their security. (SWB)

Recent publications: *Les Médias du Génocide* (Karthala/RSF, 1995, 397pp); *The Return Home — Rumours and Realities* (AI, February 1996, 63pp); *Killing the Evidence — Murder, Attacks, Arrests and Intimidation of Survivors and Witnesses* (African Rights, March 1996, 91pp)

SAUDI ARABIA

On 8 April the BBC's Arabic Service television was taken off air. The decision to halt the service — produced by the BBC and carried on a satellite owned by the Saudi company Orbit — came less than a week after a BBC programme revived criticisms of human rights abuses in Saudi Arabia. In January it emerged ' that reports on the BBC's Arabic Service about the UK government's plan to deport Mohammed al-Mas'ari to Dominica were being blacked out at Orbit's satellite relay station in Rome. At that time the BBC said the gaps in transmission were being 'urgently investigated' but it hoped the service could continue. On 9 April Orbit, owned by the Mawarid Group of Saudi Arabia whose chairman is the Saudi prince Khalid bin Abd al-Rahman, announced that it had 'unilaterally terminated' its contract with the BBC following what it claimed were 'many attempts to persuade the BBC to be more sensitive'. The BBC stated that both parties 'had given notice of their intention' to terminate the service. The BBC's contract specified that it should maintain editorial control of the channel's output but signs had been growing in recent months of Saudi unease over the agreement and programme content. (*Guardian, Independent*)

SERBIA-MONTENEGRO

Serbia: On 23 February the Supreme Court annulled the registration of the **Soros Fund of Yugoslavia**, meaning that the Fund has no right to operate, conduct financial transactions or pursue projects. The Fund had given assistance to the independent media as well as running aid programmes focusing on educational and cultural activities and had repeatedly been attacked as anti-Serb in pro-government media. (AIM, Reuter)

Nasa Borba reported on 4 March that since the government takeover of **NTV Studio B** (*Index* 2/1996) the station has begun to endorse uncritically the policies of President Milosevic and his Socialist Party of Serbia (SPS), and gave more coverage to the SPS Congress of 2 March than any other station, apart from the state-run TV and radio stations. (OMRI)

In March **Vuk Draskovic**, leader of the Serbian Renewal Movement, came under fire from state-run media for sending a letter to the foreign ministers of Russia, UK, France, Germany, Italy and the USA accusing President Milosevic of 'consolidating a one-party dictatorship'. *Vecernji Novisti* called on prosecutors to file charges against him to protect Serbia from attacks by foreign powers. Draskovic has been labelled 'the number-one enemy of the state'. (OMRI)

The Belgrade District Public Prosecutor's Office applied for permission on 3 April to investigate allegations against **Zoran Djindjic**, chairman of the Democratic Party, on charges of exposing Serbian prime minister Mirko Marjanovic to public mockery. The allegations relate to an advertisement placed in *Telegraf* which accused Marjanovic and his ministers of abusing their official position to buy low-priced wheat and sell it at a huge profit. Djindjic could be charged with committing a criminal offence against the reputation of the Republic of Serbia. (SWB)

Montenegro: On 11 March the Montenegrin PEN Club protested at the 'Serbianisation' of the Montenegrin language in the military and police force and aspects of political, social and economic life. The Club objects to the preference given to the Ekavian variant of the language, spoken in Serbia, over the Montenegrin Ijekavian language. (OMRI)

Kosovo: On 27 February **Faik Jashari**, a school principal in Batllava, was interrogated by police about his political activities. The same day police interrogated students **Bedri** and **Arben Rudari** from Shajkovc village for five hours about the lessons in their schools and reportedly threatened them with 'liquidation' if they did not leave Kosovo. According to the Council for the Defence of Human Rights and Freedoms (CDHRF) the authorities are conducting a campaign to intimidate young Albanians into leaving Kosovo. (CDHRF)

The Albanian news agency ATA reported on 9 March that Serbian authorities in Pristina have changed the Albanian names of 450 roads and squares, and that there is only one sign left in Albanian. (SWB)

CDHRF chairman **Adem Demaci** (*Index* 2/1990) was detained for two hours at a police station in Hani i Elezit on 15 March after attempting to cross the border into Macedonia on his way to Brussels to deliver a speech to the European Parliament. Documents, photographs and videotapes on human rights abuses in Kosovo were confiscated. (SWB, OMRI)

On 1 April the abolition of exit visas for Kosovo Albanians took effect. Previously Kosovars travelling via Macedonia to Albania without an exit visa risked imprisonment by Serbian authorities if they had Albanian stamps in their passports. (OMRI)

The weekly *Koha* was suspended by order of the Prosecutor General's Office for three days after its 7 April edition carried a photomontage depicting President Milosevic standing next to Nazi-uniformed soldiers under the caption 'Anschluss 1989'. Regional autonomy for Kosovo was revoked in 1989. (CPJ, HRW)

SINGAPORE

In March information minister George Yeo announced new measures against the Internet, which he described as 'an anti-pollution measure in cyberspace'. The Singapore Broadcasting Authority will monitor websites by sampling incoming material, while all service providers and organisations putting religious and political information on the Internet would be obliged to register with the SBA. In places where public Internet access is offered, such as libraries and cybercafes, software blocking access to 'objectionable' sites would have to be installed. Similarly, foreign electronic newspapers looking for local subscribers would have to register and become subject to legal conditions analogous to local newspapers. (*Straits Times*, Newsbytes News Network, Reuter)

SLOVAKIA

Parliament passed several amendments to the Penal Code on 26 March forbidding 'subversive' rallies and the dissemination of false information about Slovakia abroad. Justice minister Jozef Liscak said that 'such a law has been needed for a long time' and that similar laws exist in 'developed democratic countries'. Opposition leaders firmly condemned the new measures as vaguely defined and excessively broad, and Catholic bishops warned that law enforcement officials would be personally morally responsible for any injustices that were committed under the new law. On 4 April President Michal Kovac refused to sign the amended Penal Code and returned it to Parliament for reconsideration. (SWB)

SOUTH AFRICA

The minister of posts and telecommunications, **Pallo Jordan**, was dismissed from his post on 28 March, after a series of clashes with high-ranking members of the ANC, including President Mandela. The most notable was Jordan's opposition to state interference in broadcasting services which brought him into conflict with the deputy president, Thabo Mbeki, after Mbeki's request for a one-hour programming slot for the government on South African Broadcasting Corporation (SABC) television. (CPJ)

SOUTH KOREA

Customs agents at Kimpo International Airport seized around 200 items from North Korea found in the luggage of Mun Ho-keun on 20 February. Mun was carrying gifts given to his mother, **Pak Yong-kil**, during her unauthorised visit to North Korea last summer (*Index* 5/1995, 6/1995, 1/1996). They included North Korean propaganda material, a ring, medicine, and pottery. (SWB)

On 26 February **Bruce Cheesman**, Seoul correspondent for the *Australian Financial Review*, was refused a renewal of his work visa. Cheesman is currently writing an unauthorised biography of President Kim Young-sam. The South Korean embassy in Australia has made several complaints about Cheesman's reports and defamation proceedings have recently been initiated as a result of his

portrayal of the president. (Reuter, *Financial Times*, *Independent*)

The reappointment of Kang Sung-koo as president of the Munhwa Broadcasting Corporation on 13 March was criticised by journalists as politically motivated. Union leaders at the station claimed that the government was aiming to use the network to gain electoral advantage in the run-up to parliamentary elections on 11 April. Munhwa is the second-largest broadcaster in the country with affiliate stations in 19 cities. At least 112 people were arrested on charges of violating election law during the 16-day campaign. President Kim, whose New Korea Party lost its overall majority in the National Assembly but remains the largest party, has warned that 'a considerable number' of new members could lose their seats in Parliament if they are found to have broken the electoral law. (Reuter)

Recent publications: *Update on National Security Law Arrests and Ill-Treatment — The Need for Human Rights Reform* (AI, March 1996, 6pp); *Open Letter to Political Parties on the Occasion of the April 1996 National Assembly Elections* (AI, February 1996, 5pp)

SRI LANKA

On 26 February a military court of enquiry found 14 soldiers, all privates and lance-corporals, guilty of killing 24 Tamil civilians and wounding 26 others during a raid on the village of Kumarapuram, eastern Trincomalee district, on 11 February. The government acknowledges that more than 50,000 people have been killed since 1983 in the civil war. (AI, Reuter)

The government imposed an indefinite ban on news broadcasts by **MBC Networks**, a private radio network, on 9 April. Sirasa FM, one of its stations, had announced a non-existent islandwide curfew. Two journalists from the station were charged with bringing the government into disrepute and broadcasting false news. The Editors' Guild of Sri Lanka said the punishment was in excess of the crime and noted that the radio station had corrected the item within seven minutes. On 19 April all local media were forbidden from covering military affairs, in the wake of a fresh government assault on Tamil separatists in the north. (Reuter)

Recent publication: *Silent War — Censorship and the Conflict in Sri Lanka* (A19, March 1996, 63pp)

SWEDEN

US director **Martin Scorsese** has given way to the National Board of Film Censors' decision to cut three scenes, totalling one minute 40 seconds, from his new film *Casino*. He has asked the film's Swedish distributor to precede screenings with the message: 'It was my wish that each audience should experience the film as I cut it, but that was not to be, and a censored version seems a better alternative than not showing

the film at all.' (Reuter)

TAIWAN

Human rights groups have criticised media coverage of the country's first free elections, held on 23 March, as politically biased. Taiwan's three licensed television stations are all owned by the leading Kuomintang party and monitoring groups say that President Lee received four to five times more coverage than his competitors, much of it unpaid for. Although a private television company supporting the rival Democratic Progressive Party was granted a licence last year, prohibitive capitalisation requirements have kept it off the air so far. (CPJ, *Taiwan Communiqué*)

TAJIKISTAN

Victor Nikulin, a correspondent for Russian state television ORT, was shot dead in his office in Dushanbe on 28 March. Nikulin is the 29th journalist to be killed in Tajikistan since 1992. (CPJ, OMRI)

THAILAND

The conflict between the government of prime minister Banharn Silpa-archa and the **Creative Media Foundation** (CMF) intensified during February and March. On 7 February, the prime minister's office criticised the CMF discussion programme *Mong Tang Moon* ('Different Perspectives'), which led to its ban the following week. On 19 February six radio programmes hosted by the presenter of *Mong Tang Moon*,

Chirmsak Pinthong, were ordered to be taken off the air. Finally, on 3 March, the prime minister's office admitted it had banned an episode of *Vethi Chao Ban* ('Folk's Forum'). (*Bangkok Post, Far Eastern Economic Review*)

On 6 March the Thai Embassy in London confirmed the release of **Ye Gyang** and his wife (*Index* 1/1996). They were sent to a 'safe area' in Ratchaburi province for those who are considered to be vulnerable if they return to Burma. (PEN)

Saengchai Sunthornwat, head of the Mass Communications Organisation of Thailand (MCOT) and a columnist for the daily *Thai Rath*, was shot dead near his home in Bangkok on 11 April. MCOT controls two television stations, nine radio stations and the Thai News Agency. Saengchai had recently cancelled several music programmes on Channel 9 television, and it is thought that his murder could be connected with the decision. (CPJ)

TIBET

The Committee of Nationalities and Religious Affairs announced on 15 February that it will close politically problematic lamaseries and jail separatist monks and nuns. According to the official *Tibet Daily* the Committee has called for tighter management of lamaseries and education on patriotism and socialism for monks, nuns, and lay Buddhists. (Reuter)

An open letter to Yaşar Kemal from Arthur Miller

On 5 April 1996 PEN American Center released an open letter from US playwright Arthur Miller to his friend and colleague, the Turkish writer Yaşar Kemal

DEAR YAŞAR,

Your current crisis reminds me of the pleasurable hours in your home when with Harold Pinter I learned so much about Turkey from your sharp yet tolerant observations. And earlier in our meetings in Khirgizia, when with my wife Ingeborg Morath, along with writers from so many places on the earth we experienced the incredible hour when Gorbachev first seemed to be opening up Russia to the world. Do you recall our cautious hopefulness that perhaps the road ahead might be climbing toward a new vista of freedom, not only for Russians but the world? At last the end of the waste of human energy and talent and creativity that was the cold war!

Now, as I understand it, you have a judicial sentence hanging over your head should you ever utter another word in defence of your own people. Knowing your love of Turkey and the Turkish people as well as the Kurds, you must be stunned by this action.

In this age, when we send our thoughts anywhere at the touch of a button, you are forbidden, on pain of imprisonment, of letting certain thoughts past your lips. What a painful absurdity! And what power is coiled in this evil seed of suppression that it can be destroyed, so it would seem, in one country only to rise on the wind to sprout again in another! If it were not so serious it would be a theme for a comedy, a farce, in fact. But of course farce is not at all what this is for you and for human freedom.

Yaşar, dear friend, there are people everywhere in the world who know you through your books and their life-affirming humanity, people who are with you in spirit now. I am sure they look upon this repression with incredulity if not anger and disgust, and salute you with the greatest respect.

Your friend, Arthur Miller

A culture denied

by Nicole Pope

'I condemn you,' shouted a furious Yaşar Kemal to his judges, as he stormed out of Istanbul State Security Court on 7 March. The court had handed down a 20-month suspended jail sentence for violating Article 312 of the penal code by 'inciting racial hatred by displaying ethnic and regional differences'. Kemal had been tried for the publication of an article on the Kurdish question in a Turkish collection of essays entitled *Freedom of Thought and Turkey.*

Kemal — sometimes described as the 'the most Turkish of Kurdish writers or the most Kurdish of Turkish writers' — is no stranger to controversy. His forcefully expressed views have brought him trouble with the law several times. 'The first time, I was in secondary school. We were talking about land reform. I was arrested and severely beaten up,' he explains. From then on, he was labelled a 'Communist' by the authorities and was arrested several times.

As a young boy, growing up in a Turkish village of the Cukurova region he was fascinated by the story-tellers who travelled from hamlet to hamlet, recounting for the spell-bound villagers ancient tales and epic legends drawn from the rich culture of the Turkmen tribes that had peopled the region. His family, as a feudal Kurdish family, even had its own *dengbej* (a Kurdish bard) who would tell epics in verse, drawn from the Kurdish culture. As soon as he was old enough, Kemal accompanied these men and started to collect stories from the regional folklore. 'My first book was a collection of elegies. I had collected 500 or perhaps 1,000 of them. Some were published in 1943, some were given to the Turkish Language Institute in Ankara. Those I had kept at home were confiscated by the police.'

The heroic feats described in traditional tales were a source of great inspiration for Kemal's own novels, which often depict larger-than-life characters dealt hard blows by a tragic fate. Like the story-tellers of his childhood, he aspires above all to pass on the rich popular language of the countryside. 'Our Pushkin, Nazim Hikmet, was the first of a new generation of poets who, although they may have lived in cities, used popular literature as a source of inspiration. Nazim was from Istanbul, he was an aristocrat. He met the people for the first time in prison. That's where he got to know the richness of the language, of the popular culture.'

Kemal was surprised by the strong outbursts in the nationalist press that followed publication of his two articles. 'It was like an explosion,' he says. The fact that the essays had been published abroad seems to have been a major irritant, but he also believes overreaction is due to a more acute sensitivity to the Kurdish issue.

Although Kemal claims to be the 'most cowardly man in every day life', he is determined not to be intimidated and to continue speaking out for an end to the bloody conflict that has been tearing Turkey apart for the past 12 years. 'In my view, this war is stupid. I don't believe the Kurds, if they obtained cultural rights, would want independence,' he says. 'But 3.5 million people have been evacuated from their villages, more than 4,000 have been assassinated, acres of forests have been burnt, wheat fields destroyed. Even worse, a food embargo is imposed on some villages,' he adds. 'I told Mesut Yilmaz, when he came to see me [before the December elections]: if the war goes on, Turkey will face serious problems in the future; but if you can solve this problem, it will have democracy.'

Recently, he has seen some encouraging signs. 'The new left is now taking a position against the war. The Alevis are against it. Progressive people, even businessmen are now speaking up. The influence of civil society will be felt more and more, because the conflict is so costly.'

Kemal does not want to be categorised as nationalist, Kurdish or Turkish. Brought up in both traditions — although he writes only in Turkish — he would like to see the cultures of Anatolia coexist peacefully. 'I believe the world is like a garden with thousands of colours, thousands of cultures,' he says. 'If the Kurdish culture, if the Circassian, Arab, Syriac, Chaldean cultures could survive, Anatolia could again, as in the past, contribute new shades to the universal culture.'

Nicole Pope *is* Le Monde*'s correspondent in Turkey*

Recent publication: *Cutting Off the Serpent's Head — Tightening Control in Tibet 1994-1995* (Tibet Information Network and HRW/Asia, March 1996, 192pp)

TONGA

Filokalafi Akau'ola, acting editor of the *Times of Tonga*, and journalist Filini Sikuea were found guilty of 'angering a civil servant' on 15 April and ordered to be of good behaviour for 18 months and one year respectively. The men were charged in connection with letters published in the paper calling for democracy in Tonga. The police minister, Clive Edwards, was apparently angered at the contents of the letters. Akau'ola and Sikuea are to appeal. (SWB)

TRINIDAD & TOBAGO

Pressure on staff at the *Trinidad Guardian* has increased in recent months. After the prime minister, Basdeo Panday, lifted a temporary ban on the paper's access to government information n February, the Trinidad Publishing Company (TPC), which publishes the *Guardian*, started inspecting each issue prior to publication and demanding alterations. On 1 April the paper's managing director, Alwin Chow, was dismissed after telling his staff that the ANSA McAl conglomerate, which owns TPC, was pressing him to sack columnist Hulsie Bhaggan, over a column she wrote in mid-March criticising attorney-general Ramesh Lawrence Maharaj. ANSA McAl also wanted to vet copy

in advance of publication, he said, and to make sure that nothing was published about the religious group Jamaat-al-Muslimeen, which staged a failed coup in 1990 and whose members Maharaj had represented in court. The editors and several staff journalists resigned in protest at the interference and at Chow's dismissal. (CCPJ, *Trinidad Express*)

TURKEY

On 7 March Yaşar Kemal was given a 20-month sentence, suspended for five years, by the State Security Court of Istanbul. He was convicted of 'inciting racism' under Article 312 of the Criminal Code, in connection with two articles entitled *More Oppression* and *The Dark Cloud over Turkey* (*Index* 1/1995, p141). His publisher, Erdal Öz, was given a suspended fine. Kemal's lawyers plan to appeal to the Turkish courts and, if necessary, to the European Court of Human Rights. (*Index* 1/1995, 2/1995, 2/1996). (PEN, RSF)

On 15 March, Istanbul police detained eight people associated with the left-wing daily *Atilim* (*Index* 6/1995). The paper's editor-in-chief, Ibrahim Cicek; his wife, Fusun Erdogdu; Haci Orman, a journalist on the paper's foreign desk; Ali Hidir Polat, a poet and journalist; Aslihan Yucesan, *Atilim*'s owner; and staff members Sabahat Karahan, Zeynet Yesil and Duran Sahin are thought to have been detained because *Atilim* banners were seen at a 12 March

commemoration of 1995 riots in Istanbul. On 19 March, the State Security Court closed *Atilim* for one month for 'separatist propaganda'. Ismail Akkin, the daily's editor, was sentenced to six months in prison on the same charge. He is currently free pending an appeal. The order also suspended *Özgür Genclik*, a magazine published by *Atilim*. On 26 March they were all charged with 'belonging to the MLKP (the banned Marxist-Leninist party)'. Sabahat Karahan and Aslihan Yucesan have since been released. (RSF, CPJ)

Between 13 and 21 March a series of arrests and detentions of journalists took place. Erhan Duman, Bülent Senlik and Hamza Yalcin of the *Odak Review* were detained and accused of being members of an illegal organisation. An arrest warrant was issued against Emine Durmus of *Özgür Genclik*. Özgür Saltik of *Partizanin Sesi* was detained and tortured, while Hüsniye Akbulut of the same publication was sentenced to one year in prison and fined. Fehmi Isik, Ibrahim Halil Dede and Mehmet Eren of *Rohani* were detained by police and copies of *Rohani* seized. Hatun Temizalp of *Proleter Halkin Birligi* and Serpil Kermaz of *Demokrasi* were also detained. And on 21 March Gönca Dönmezer, an employee of *Kizil Bayrak*, was arrested and beaten by police during a Newroz (Kurdish New Year) demonstration. (IFJ, RSF)

On 23 March police beat several journalists,

photographers and cameramen covering a police raid on an Ankara University building which had been taken over by students protesting increases in tuition fees. **Burhan Özbilici**, a photographer with Associated Press, **Kemal Gökcanli**, a cameraman for Channel 6 television, and **Serkan Cinier**, a cameraman for Interstar television, were assaulted. **Meryem Akpinar** of *Atilim* and **Cengis Aslan** of *Gencligin Sesi* were beaten and subsequently taken into custody. (CPJ, RSF)

On 9 April Istanbul State Security Court ordered the daily *Evrensel* to close for one month in connection with two articles published in August 1995 which 'incited racial hatred by way of regional and racial discrimination' and included 'statements by a terrorist organisation'. **Ali Erol**, the paper's editor, was sentenced to two years in prison and fined US$1,050 on the same charges. Erol remains free and the paper continues publishing pending appeals. *Evrensel* had also been ordered to close for one month on 4 April for 'inciting hatred' and 'promoting racism' in a September 1995 article about World Peace Day. The editors claim that the cases were brought in retaliation for the paper's determination to follow up on the death in custody of its reporter **Metin Göktepe** (*Index* 2/1996). Eleven police officers are to be tried for murder and more than 30 officers for lesser charges relating to Göktepe's death. (CPJ)

Recent publications: *Information on Continuing Human Rights Abuses* (AI, February 1996, 19pp); *Thinking is a Crime — Report on Freedom of Expression in Turkey* (International Association for Human Rights in Kurdistan, Marhc 1996, 52pp)

UNITED KINGDOM

Raghbir Singh (*Index* 3/1995), who has been detained without charge or trial since 29 March 1995, had his application for judicial review and habeas corpus rejected by the High Court on 16 February. (AI)

The chief immigration adjudicator ordered the Home Office to reconsider Saudi dissident **Mohammed al-Mas'ari**'s claim for asylum on 6 March (*Index* 2/1996). He accused ministers of trying to 'circumvent for diplomatic and trade reasons' the government's obligations under the 1951 UN Convention on Refugees. The Home Office announced on 18 April that al-Mas'ari would be granted exceptional leave to remain in the country for four years, but he would not be granted full asylum. (*Guardian, Times, Independent*)

A campaigner for the legalisation of cannabis was jailed for 12 months after writing and publishing a guide on growing the drug at home. **Michael Marlow** was convicted on 19 March by Worcester Crown Court of inciting others to produce cannabis. The judge told Marlow that his book was a guide to break, rather than change, the law. (*Times*)

The national heritage secretary, Virginia Bottomley, announced on 25 March that in light of recent technological developments the government will seek to amend the Broadcasting Bill in order to prevent foreign political organisations from beaming propaganda into their countries from satellite links based in Britain. 'Political organisations have never been allowed to own a broadcasting licence, and it has always been an offence under broadcasting legislation to broadcast material which incites to crime or disorder or is offensive to public feeling' (*Index* 2/1996, p14). (Department of National Heritage)

On 27 March the European Court of Human Rights began hearing a challenge by **Nigel Wingrove**, director of the film *Visions of Ecstasy*, against the UK's blasphemy laws. The film, an interpretation of the religious-erotic visions of St Theresa, was refused a certificate by the British Board of Film Classification in 1989 on the grounds of blasphemy. Salman Rushdie, in a written submission to the Court, said that the 'anachronistic' blasphemy laws set up intellectual 'no-go areas'. (Reuter, *Independent*)

The right of journalists to protect their sources was upheld by the European Court of Human Rights on 27 March, when they ruled in favour of **Bill Goodwin**, formerly a journalist with the *Engineer*, who was fined in 1990 for refusing to reveal his sources for a story (*Index* 2/1990, 6/1990). Section 10 of the Contempt of Court Act allows judges to order disclosure of sources where this is necessary for reasons of national security, the prevention of crime or 'in the interests of justice' (the basis of Goodwin's punishment). The European Court ruled that this wording is too broad. (*Guardian, Times, Independent*)

The High Court granted the Department of Trade and Industry an injunction banning *The Economist* from publishing further details from a leaked report by the Monopolies and Mergers Commission on 16 April. The report, part of which was published in the magazine the previous week, dealt with a proposed take-over in the electricity industry. (*Guardian, Economist*)

Recent publication: *Wrongful Detention of Asylum-Seeker Raghbir Singh* (AI, February 1996, 10pp)

USA

On 17 February a federal judge in Philadelphia blocked the government from enforcing the indecency provision of the **Telecommunications Act**, following the ACLU's suit against the government (*Index* 2/1996). The law imposes fines of up to US$250,000 and up to six years in prison for those who knowingly make available indecent material over interactive computer services to anyone under 18. On 6 March another suit was filed against the Telecommunications Act by Microsoft and all the major online services as well as many more traditional information

providers such as the American Library, Booksellers and Newspaper Associations. The suit argues that the Internet deserves First Amendment protections at least as broad as those afforded to print media and contends that individual users and parents, not the government, should determine what comes into their homes (see below). (*International Herald Tribune, Media Daily*)

On 8 March chief executives of the television industry met President Clinton in Washington with a rating plan scheduled to go into effect next January, which will work with the new **v-chip** screening technology (*Index* 1/1996). The industry says the agreement was 'totally voluntary' with 'no government involvement of any kind'. However, the agreement comes after considerable political pressure from the Clinton administration, and it has been suggested that the v-chip and rating system has been accepted as part of a 'trade-off' in return for the lucrative expansion of available channels contained in the Telecommunications Act. (*Media Daily*)

On 13 March **Markus Wolf**, the former East German spymaster, was denied a visa to enter the US by the State Department because of his previous involvement with state-sponsored terrorism. Wolf was planning to visit Random House, who are publishing the US edition of his autobiography. Wolf, who headed the Stasi's foreign espionage operations, denies

that he was directly involved with terrorism. (*Times*)

On March 14 basketball star **Mahmoud Abdul-Rauf** was banned from the NBA for refusing to stand for the national anthem. Abdul-Rauf, who was known as Chris Jackson before his conversion to Islam, is a guard for the Denver Nuggets. 'My duty is to my creator not to nationalistic ideology,' he said. On 16 March, however, Abdul-Rauf agreed to stand for the national anthem if he could pray during it. 'In Islam, if after making a decision you see that which is better, you do that,' he said. (*Times*)

The American Episcopalian Church began its first heresy trial for more than 70 years in March in St John's Cathedral, Wilmington, Delaware. Retired bishop **Walter Righter** is on trial for ordaining the New Jersey priest Barry Stopfel in 1990, despite knowing he was a practising homosexual. Bishop Righter argues that the 1979 anti-homosexual convention adopted by the Church's General Convention does not constitute doctrine but was merely a 'recommendation'. (*Times*)

On 4 April the World Wide Web consortium announced that it will have a protocol available later in the year to enable parents to monitor what their children can access. The new standard Platform for Internet Content Selection (PICS) has the backing of 39 firms including Microsoft and Netscape, and has been developed in order to avert the threat of censorship of the Internet feed. (*Computer Weekly*)

Congress passed new anti-terrorism legislation on 19 April. The bill contains summary exclusion provisions that will deny people who arrive in the country without proper documentation the right to apply for asylum, as well as changes to the appeal process for death row inmates, sharply limiting the rights of federal judges to overturn capital sentences passed by state courts. Observers believe the law will lead to a significant rise in the number of death sentences carried out. President Clinton has said he will sign the bill into law, despite misgivings about some of its provisions. (AI, *Independent*)

ZAMBIA

Bright Mwape and **Fred M'membe**, editors of the independent daily the *Post*, and columnist **Lucy Sichone** were found guilty of contempt of Parliament on 23 February by the speaker, Robinson Nabulyto (*Index* 2/1996). Nabulyto sentenced the three to indefinite prison terms and ordered them to apologise, sparking condemnation from the UN Human Rights Committee and international human rights groups. The accused immediately went into hiding, and a reward of 2 million Kwachas (US$2,000) was offered for their capture. On the morning of 4 March M'membe and Mwape handed themselves in, but Sichone remained at large. On 12 March it was reported that a student debating association at the University of Zambia had been banned by the dean of the students' union after it issued a press release criticising the indefinite sentences. On 27 March, after 24 days detention in maximum security jails, Mwape and M'membe were released following a challenge to their arrest mounted by their lawyer, Sakwiba Sikota, under a writ of habeas corpus. (IPS, MISA, CPJ, *Mail & Guardian*, *Southern Africa Report*)

Recent publication: *A Human Rights Review Based on the International Covenant on Civil and Political Rights* (AI, March 1996, 13pp)

ZIMBABWE

Financial Gazette editor **Trevor Ncube** was sacked on 2 March by Elias Rusike, chief executive of the paper's parent company, Modus Publications. Ncube is well known for his exposés of government corruption and incompetence. His removal from office and the subsequent muzzling of the *Financial Gazette* meant that the campaign for presidential elections held in mid-March was reported solely by newspapers that support the ruling Zanu (PF) party. (*Times*)

★ ★ ★

General publications: *Directory of African Media* edited by Adewale Maja-Pearce (IFJ, January 1996, 384pp); '*Why Do Ruling Classes Fear History?*' *and Other Questions* by Harvey J Kaye (Macmillan, 1996, 270pp); *1996 UN Commission on Human Rights*

— *Recommendations on Countries on the Agenda* (AI, March 1996, 29pp); *Women's Rights are Human Rights — Commitments made by Governments in the Beijing Declaration and the Platform for Action* (AI, March 1996, 28pp); *Attacks on the Press in 1995* (CPJ, March 1996, 300pp)

★ ★★

Compiled by: Anna Feldman, Lara Pawson, Kate Thal (*Africa*); Nathalie de Broglio, Dagmar Schlüter, James Solomon (*Americas*); Nicholas McAulay, Mansoor Mirza, Sarah Smith, Saul Venit (*Asia*); Laura Bruni, Robin Jones, Vera Rich (*eastern Europe and CIS*); Michaela Becker, Philippa Nugent (*Middle East*); Ian Franklin, Predrag Zivkovic (*western Europe*)

• **CHINA** The report mentioned in *Index* 2/1996 (page 162) was incorrectly credited to Human Rights Watch/Asia. The correct reference is to Human Rights in China's report Caught Between Tradition and the State: Violations of the Human Rights of Chinese Women (*August 1995*)

ANDRES SERRANO Piss Christ *1987, cibachrome, silicone, plexiglass, wood frame, 60x40"*

USA: Art unleashed

A desire to marry art and politics
figures prominently in the
contemporary US art scene.
This least censored of all means of
expression has become the vehicle for
voices otherwise excluded or
marginalised by mainstream society:
what Edward Lucie-Smith calls
'a megaphone for the dispossessed'

ROGER KIMBALL

Uncensored and unashamed

The idea that art, or any other form of expression, is censored in the USA today is preposterous. In testing the limits of free expression, artists have trivialised not only art but the freedom in whose name it was created

A NYONE with a taste for absurdity will find much to admire in the more 'advanced' precincts of the contemporary art world. There are, first of all, the many grotesque elements of the spectacle: government-funded 'performance' artists (or do I mean performance 'artists'?) who smear themselves with chocolate and then prance about haranguing their audiences about the evils of patriarchy, capitalism, etc (Karen Finley); conceptual artists who conceal themselves under a false floor in an art gallery, masturbating continuously for hours on end while broadcasting their sighs and whispers to gallery-goers who tread unknowingly above them (Vito Acconci); pathetic figures, like the chap whose most famous piece featured himself nailed to an automobile (Chris Burden); and then there are the miscellaneous knaves and charlatans of all description, the battalions of eager hucksters who make up for their lack of talent and artistic accomplishment with a combination of egotism, shamelessness and an acute sense of marketing.

The cornucopia of absurdity that the art world has become offers hours of entertainment to the student of human fatuousness. Not, of course, that all artists contribute to this degraded and degrading sideshow. But here we must distinguish quite sharply between the serious life of art, which pursues its own course, and the chic purlieus of the 'cutting-edge', which are corrupted by a rebarbative academic hermeticism on the one side and an addiction to extremity on the other. It is of course cutting-edge art that gets all the attention, that infests the galleries of SoHo and TriBeCa (and Cork Street), that garners grants from the National Endowment of the Arts, and gets written up in reader-proof journals like *Artforum* and *October*. If there were a nationwide moratorium on the use of words like 'transgressive', denizens of the art world would be instantly out of business. For what they traffic in is not art but a species of cultural politics that poaches on the authority of art in order, first, to enhance its prestige (and its prices) and, second, to purchase immunity from certain forms of criticism.

To a large extent, the calamities of art today are due to the aftermath of the avant-garde: to all those 'adversarial' gestures, poses, ambitions and tactics that emerged and were legitimised in the 1880s and 1890s, flowered in the first half of this century, and that live a sort of posthumous existence now in the frantic twilight of postmodernism. In part, our present situation, like avant-garde itself, is a complication (not to say a perversion) of our Romantic inheritance. The elevation of art from a didactic pastime to a prime spiritual resource, the self-conscious probing of inherited forms and artistic strictures, the image of the artist as a tortured, oppositional figure: all achieve a first maturity in Romanticism. These themes were exacerbated as the avant-garde developed from an impulse to a movement and finally into a tradition of its own.

The French critic Albert Thibaudet summarised some of the chief features of this burgeoning tradition in his reflections on the Symbolist movement in literature. Writing in 1936, Thibaudet noted that Symbolism 'accustomed literature to the idea of indefinite revolution' and inaugurated a 'new climate' in French literature: a climate characterised by 'the chronic avant-gardism of poetry, the "What's new?" of the "informed" public ... the proliferation of schools and manifestos,' and the ambition 'to occupy that extreme point, to attain for an hour that crest of the wave in a tossing sea. The Symbolist revolution,' Thibaudet concluded, 'might perhaps have been definitively the last, because it incorporated the theme of chronic revolution into the normal condition of literature.' The problem is that the avant-garde has become a casualty of its own success. Having won battle after battle, it gradually transformed a recalcitrant bourgeois culture into a willing collaborator in its raids on established taste. But in this victory were the seeds of its own irrelevance, for without credible resistance, its oppositional gestures degenerated into a kind of aesthetic buffoonery. In this sense, the institutionalisation of the avant-garde — what the critic Clement Greenberg called 'avant-gardism' — spells the death, or at least the senility, of the avant-garde.

As the search for something new to say or do becomes ever more desperate, artists push themselves to make extreme gestures simply in order to be noticed. But an inexorably self-defeating logic has taken hold here: at a time when so much art is routinely extreme and audiences have become inured to the most brutal spectacles, extremity itself becomes a commonplace. After one has had oneself nailed to a Volkswagen, what's left? Having oneself nailed to a Rolls Royce? A Chevy? A Volvo? A Citroën? Without the sustaining, authoritative backdrop of the normal, extreme gestures — stylistic, moral, political — degenerate into a grim species of mannerism. Lacking any guiding aesthetic imperative, such gestures, no matter how shocking or repulsive they may be, are so many exercises in futility.

It is in part to compensate for this encroaching futility that the desire to marry art and politics has become such a prominent feature of the contemporary art scene. When the artistic significance of art is at a minimum, politics rushes in to fill the void. From the crude political allegories of a Leon Golub or Hans Haacke to the feminist sloganeering of Jenny Holzer, Karen Finley, or Cindy Sherman, much that goes under the name of art today is incomprehensible without reference to its political content. Indeed, in many cases what we see are nothing but political gestures that poach on the prestige of art in order to enhance their authority. Another word for this activity is propaganda, although at a moment when so much of art is given over to propagandising the word seems inadequate. It goes without saying that the politics in question are as predictable as clockwork. Not only are they standard items on the prevailing tablet of left-wing pieties, they are also cartoon versions of the same. It's the political version of painting by numbers: AIDS, the homeless, 'gender politics', the Third World and the environment line up on one side with white hats, while capitalism, patriarchy, the United States and traditional morality and religion assemble yonder in black hats.

It is in this context that we must understand the outcry over 'censorship' and freedom of expression in the American art world. I employ scare quotes because the idea that art — or any other form of expression, for that matter — is censored in the US today is preposterous. Take a trip to the local news-stand; turn on the television to MTV or any

KAREN FINLEY The American Chestnut, *1995*

of a number of 'adult' channels; visit the Biennial exhibition of the Whitney Museum of American Art: anywhere and everywhere in American society the foulest possible language, the most graphic images of sexual congress and sexual perversion, the most inflammatory speech ridiculing political and religious leaders abounds. The heavy hand of government is happy to regulate smoking and the composition of potato crisps; it interferes not a whit with what artists and *soi-disants* artists may say or represent in their art.

And yet we again and again hear that the freedom of artists is threatened. How can this be? The controversy crystallised a few years ago over two photographers, Andres Serrano and Robert Mapplethorpe. Serrano achieved instant celebrity for *Piss Christ*, a photograph of a crucifix submerged in Mr Serrano's urine. Mapplethorpe, as all the world knows, captured the limelight with his photographs of the sadomasochistic homosexual underworld. What initially sparked controversy was not the existence or circulation of these images, but the fact that their exhibition had been partly underwritten by the National Endowment for the Arts, a governmental agency. After all, such blasphemous and perverted images had been circulating in the American art world for years with nary a raised eyebrow. But the revelation that these and other similar productions were being supported in part by taxpayers' dollars created a sensation.

It really was extraordinary. Overnight, it seemed, we were asked to believe that denying someone a government grant was tantamount to censorship and constituted a dangerous assault on the First Amendment. The mandarins of the art world really had a field day. In 1991, for example, *Art Journal*, an official organ of the College Art Association, the largest and most important academic organisation of art teachers in the country, devoted two issues to the issue of censorship. One of the guest editors was Robert Storr, an epitome of art-world trendiness who had recently been appointed curator at the Museum of Modern Art in New York. Mr Storr's own contribution to the issue was an essay entitled 'Art, Censorship, and the First Amendment: This Is Not a Test.' You know the script: the USA is now in the grip of a fearsome right-wing effort to suppress free speech; artists are being muzzled everywhere. 'On every front,' he wrote, 'legal challenges are being made to the freedom of serious artists, clever opportunists, dedicated amateurs, and ordinary people to represent the world as they see it.' I wish that Mr Storr could have cited one ordinary citizen, let alone one 'serious artist', facing such 'challenges'. But of course he adduced none because none exist.

Instead, what Mr Storr offered readers of *Art Journal* was a species of grade-school absolutism in which anything less than total freedom is rejected as intolerable repression. Accordingly, his chief concern with the First Amendment turned on the licence to utter dirty words in public. 'In the final analysis, freedom of speech isn't so much a matter of when one may legally shout "Fire!" in a crowded theatre but whether or not one may...yell "Shit!" on stage in a publicly funded production — or "Fuck!"'

The stunning superficiality of Mr Storr's performance was summed up in his claim that 'defending free speech depends on a willingness...to break taboos when and wherever they present themselves.' It is worth pausing over this statement to contemplate what the nightmare of a society without taboos might be like. For Mr Storr, however, respecting taboos is tantamount to 'repressive decorum' and 'general self-censorship'. (Is 'self-censorship' the same thing as censorship?) In order to illustrate what he has in mind by free speech, he returns to the case of Robert Mapplethorpe, the archetypal 'transgressive artist'. Why didn't *The New York Times*, which had recently run an article about the Mapplethorpe controversy by the art critic Hilton Kramer, reproduce the offending photographs? For Mr Storr, this was an instance of 'pre-emptive and accusatory squeamishness'. To make up for the omission, he did his readers the 'courtesy' of reproducing in glossy exactness Mapplethorpe's notorious *X Portfolio*, which features grisly images of sexual torture and degradation.

If the measure of art really were its capacity to offend — as Mr Storr and so many like-minded champions of the moment have been eager to assure us — then Robert Mapplethorpe's photographs would indeed be masterpieces. But offensiveness is merely offensiveness, not an index of artistic quality. And this brings us to the two key questions with which this spurious battle over censorship confronts us.

The first issue concerns what we might call the moral status of art. It is widely assumed that by baptising something as 'art' we thereby exempt it from other kinds of criticism — as if an object's status as art rendered it invulnerable to extra-aesthetic censure. Some such assumption, for example, stands behind Oscar Wilde's famous observation that 'There is no such thing as a moral or an immoral book. Books are well written or badly written. That is all.' Like everything Wilde wrote, that is very nicely phrased; but the question remains, is it true? Is it true that Robert Mapplethorpe's depiction of one man urinating into another man's mouth should be judged purely in *aesthetic* terms? Dostoevsky once wrote that 'Beauty is the battlefield where God and the Devil war for the soul of man.' It is perhaps an open question whether Robert Mapplethorpe's photographs can lay claim to beauty; but clearly they issue a moral challenge. This is why the art critic who defended Mapplethorpe's photographs on 'formal' grounds, adducing in one instance the 'classical' disposition of the diagonals in a depiction of a man inserting his forearm

What they traffic in is not art but a species of cultural politics that poaches on the authority of art to enhance its prestige and purchase immunity from certain forms of criticism

Alarm bells

HUMAN RIGHTS WATCH is concerned about the nature of the attacks being made on the independence of — indeed, the very existence of — two federally-funded agencies that play an important role in enhancing diversity of expression in the United States: the National Endowment for the Arts (NEA) and the Corporation for Public Broadcasting (CPB).

While we believe there is an affirmative free speech value in fostering alternative voices, both in the arts and on radio and television, we take no position on whether the United States should provide public support for the arts or broadcasting, or, if such support is to be maintained, at what level. Indeed, in our experience state sponsorship of the arts in many other countries has been a vehicle for government manipulation and control.

What is remarkable about the debate over arts and broadcasting funding in the United States, however, is that the NEA and CPB are in trouble precisely because they have, over the years, been effectively insulated from political interference. The art and programming under fire is being targeted not because it serves established orthodoxies, but because it is believed to be challenging them.

The record leaves little doubt that those who would cut back or entirely defund the budgets of the NEA and CPB would do so in order to impose a political orthodoxy, or at least to suppress these challenging, alternative voices. This was demonstrated most crudely in Senator Larry Pressler's effort to probe the

into another man's rectum, was offering not criticism but a cynical exercise in nihilistic persiflage.

Which brings us to the second key question: the relationship between freedom of expression and the limits of acceptable behaviour. The two are not necessarily the same. As the philosopher John Searle has pointed out, 'From the proposition that one has a right to do something it does not follow that it is a right or even a morally permissible thing to do.' The fact that one has a legal right to engage in some behaviour does not necessarily make that behaviour acceptable. Searle continues: 'Any healthy human institution — family, state, university, ski team — grants its members rights that far exceed the bounds of morally acceptable behaviour. There are many reasons for this. One is that the flexibility necessary for free, successful and creative behaviour requires a big gulf between what the institution grants by way of rights and what it has to expect it is to political beliefs and affiliations of CPB employees. Whatever one's ultimate philosophical view of government-financed expression, these tactics should set off alarm bells.

As this debate has proceeded during the past several years, any critics of the NEA and CPB have argued that it is fundamentally unfair to have their tax dollars support expression which offends them, or with which they may disagree. But they ignore a well-established and unquestioned model for public support of expression: the public library.

While there are occasional skirmishes over items in library collections, virtually everyone across the political spectrum accepts the principle that a library should embrace a broad range of books and other materials, and no-one is calling for the government to get out of the library business. Yet considerable discretion is vested in professional librarians to make selection decisions on the basis of pedagogical and other politically-neutral criteria. Tax support for public libraries from the local to the federal level, dwarfs the relatively small budgets of the NEA and CPB, but goes virtually unquestioned because there is broad public understanding and acceptance of the need for independent libraries.

We urge lawmakers to keep this important and relevant precedent in mind as they consider the future of these two valuable agencies.

Statement of Human Rights Watch concerning attacks on the National Endowment for the Arts and the Corporation for Public Broadcasting

succeed. The gulf between the rights granted and the performance expected is bridged by the responsibility of the members.' In the art world today, the First Amendment is routinely invoked to justify or protect objects and behaviour whose entire raison d'être is to shock and discommode. These raids on the fringes of extremity have helped to transform the art world into a moral cesspool. In testing the limits of free expression, the art world has demonstrated its emancipation from all manner of social and aesthetic norms. In the process, it has trivialised not only art but also the freedom in whose name it was created. ❏

Roger Kimball is managing editor of The New Criterion *and author of* Tenured Radicals: how Politics has Corrupted Our Higher Education *(Harper Collins)*

DAVID C MENDOZA

The true cost of artistic expression

Just 68 cents buys a whole lot of culture and keeps alive the cultural diversity and hard-won, fundamental values dear to most Americans

THE SKIRMISHES over specific artists, projects and grants that we have experienced over the last five years were only the prelude to the music that we must face now — military bands, not New Music. Those attacks were aimed at destabilising the cultural establishment and laying a minefield in its midst. Whether you capitalise culture war or not, and whether you like their military metaphor or not, the forces that launched it are now in power and can advance from random sniper shots to full-fledged battle. Their objective is clear. The right — call it religious, Christian, radical, far, whatever — derides contemporary culture because it cannot abide its liberal underpinnings. Despite the marginalised status of artists and intellectuals in our society, the right correctly realises that art and ideas are powerful symbols of a society and now it desperately want its artists and intellectuals to have centre stage in academia, public radio and television, museums, theatres, media and popular culture, et al. The solution: 'privatise' the government agencies that support culture.

What exactly does 'privatise' mean? The term, used by William Bennett and Newt Gingrich when asked about the future of the National Endowment for the Arts (NEA) and National Endowment for the Humanities (NEH), can mean only one thing: end government support and eliminate the agencies that contribute to cultural programmes. Without government support, the remainder of funding is private; private foundation and corporate grants, private individual donations and members of the public buying memberships, tickets and trinkets at museum gift shops.

The growth of public support for culture at the federal, state and local level during the last three decades has promoted an even greater growth in corporate and private support. Although it can be debated whether public funding was the sole impetus for increased private funding, there is no debate that the cultural landscape of the nation today is more diverse and dynamic — ie looks much more like America — than before there was public funding. This is the real achievement of public agencies like the NEA, and this is precisely why the right wants to re-privatise culture.

Those of us who recognise this achievement as progress rather than what the right characterises as a slide into 'multicultural mediocrity', celebrate the diversity of cultural expressions now available in every corner of America. The evolution of public arts funding coincided with the civil rights movements and the right to cultural expression was a part of the prize. Before there was public funding there was no El Teatro Campesino (San Francisco), Northwest Asian-American Theatre (Seattle), Guadalupe Cultural Arts Center (San Antonio), Dance Theatre of Harlem, Ballet Hispanico (NYC). There was no Next Wave or Off-Off Broadway, no modern dance boom, gay and lesbian film festivals, new music, or folk art revival. And there was no Corpus Christi Arts Council, Bronx Council on the Arts, Orange County Arts Alliance, Kentucky Arts Council, or Virgin Islands Council on the Arts. And Bill T Jones, an African American, openly gay, HIV positive male dancer/choreographer was not on the cover of *Newsweek* and giving dance workshops in Wisconsin. Through one of their many successful language coups the right has successfully trivialised and undermined the basic concept of multiculturalism, but there, my friends and taxpayers, is what it really is. This array of unabashedly multicultural arts programmes was nurtured by US tax dollars, which, through government arts agencies and their systems of citizen peer panels, were awarded on the basis of artistic excellence and a respect for the diversity of the donors: the taxpayers.

These battles are indeed about values. The value of respect for individual and cultural diversity in a nation of native peoples and descendants of immigrants

By and large, almost everyone is a taxpayer, including non-citizens, and even some illegal immigrants. Contrary to current sound bites, taxpayers are not just the vocal minority who oppose how the NEA makes a few of its grants. The 86 people who buy tickets to see a performance artist in a small non-profit space in Minneapolis or Austin pay taxes too, and can rightfully expect that if that artist or organisation meets the standards of artistic merit as determined by the peer panels, then some of their tax pennies might be thrown back their way in the form of a grant to support the culture they choose to experience. Likewise, it is surely possible for each and every taxpayer (and their families) to find 68 cents worth (the amount of their tax bill that goes to the NEA) of art they appreciate funded by the NEA. This might include Great Performances or American Playhouse on PBS, books written by writers and published by non-profit presses, or recordings made by non-profit music groups, all funded in part by the NEA and available in virtually every congressional district of all 50 states and territories.

The right further proposes that eliminating public support is really only an end to 'welfare for the rich'. It is the thesis of political commentator George Will and others that 'those who want culture can afford to pay for it themselves.' Now the rich are also taxpayers so they might rightfully expect to have some of their nickels and dimes support the art they enjoy, and Will is probably correct in suggesting that the wealthy will not do without the arts if the NEA is axed. However, from his privileged perch among the socio-economic élite his arrogant classism is astounding. He implies that any folk who want to make or experience art can ante up their own dollars, find a Fortune 500 company and a foundation to give them grants, and if they can't raise enough to cover the costs, then set the tariff accordingly, and expect those who want to attend to pay the price. Right.

No matter what they name it or how they spin it what they really want is to force many of us back into our respective closets and re-establish the cultural landscape of the 1950s. Such a culture coup is a prize trophy in their 'battle for the soul of America'. This would be accomplished with a return to private sector support which they cynically know will not afford the diversity of expression we have begun to experience since 1960. This prize will not be won without resistance and it is forming as you read this. Even the major arts institutions (and hopefully their corporate board members) are finally taking these guys seriously. Despite this analysis, my own view is they will not ultimately win at all. This battle represents the

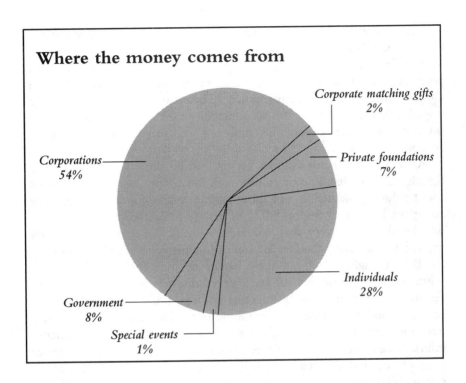

Where the money comes from

Corporate matching gifts
2%

Private foundations
7%

Corporations
54%

Individuals
28%

Government
8%

Special events
1%

last desperate gasp of an old world order at the *fin de siècle*. Late twentieth century demographics, the civil rights achievements and the impact of decades of cultural diversity, will not be erased and pushed back into any closet. However, things may certainly get worse before they get better, while they try to divert our tax dollars from supporting cultural pluralism toward building orphanages for the children of unwed teen mothers or reviving Star Wars.

In 1996 you may have an extra 68 cents in your pocket — maybe it will even be a whopping US$3 if they manage to eliminate the NEH, the Corporation for Public Broadcasting, as well as the NEA. You might send it to your local National Public Radio station during their fund drive; apply it toward a ticket to a performance or film festival, or a book of poetry. Or you could set it aside for postage stamps, phone calls, and faxes to members of Congress to tell them over and over and over that US$3 doesn't buy much culture, especially for low-income and middle-class families; and that saving every taxpayer US$3 will have an infinitesimal effect on the deficit.

A defence for the preservation of public support for culture does not preclude our efforts to hold agencies such as the NEA accountable to the Constitution and the First Amendment. These two efforts can and will be waged in tandem. Indeed, this accountability itself is a hallmark of public support, one that cannot be enforced on private foundations or corporations.

As we don our battle fatigues, let's at least be clear about what we are fighting for. The battles over culture with the 104th Congress will not be about reducing the deficit, not about ending welfare for the rich, and not about the largesse or responsibility of private philanthropy. These battles will be about the very first contracts with all Americans in all their hyphenated diversity: the Declaration of Independence, the Constitution, the Bill of Rights. And yes, these battles are indeed about values. The value of respect for individual and cultural diversity in a nation of native peoples and descendants of immigrants that is part of a world with a global economy and instantaneous communication. The value of intellectual freedom, critical thinking, and dissent in a world where fundamentalist militants and totalitarian regimes imprison and/or issue death threats against artists and assassinate journalists. The value of accepting the moral responsibility of caring for children, even if they aren't your own and even if you don't have any. The value of our environment apart from the profit to be made from its natural resources. These values may not be 'traditional' for all individuals, families, or politicians. But these are socially redeeming values, and our society is, now more than ever, desperately in need of redemption. ❏

David C Mendoza is executive director of the National Campaign for Freedom of Expression, based in Seattle, WA, and Washington, DC. This article first appeared in their newsletter, NCFE Bulletin

© David C Mendoza 1995

AMY ADLER

Photography on trial

Public anxiety over sexual expression has reached an unprecedented peak. Portrayal of childhood sexuality is at the centre of the debate

L EGAL censure of artists who indulge in sexual imagery — particularly photographers and most particularly photographers of children — has no effect on their commercial and critical success. Or does it?

It struck me as ironic that *Index* would see America as an uncensored society at precisely the time we are witnessing an era of increased censoriousness in the USA. Rising attacks on artistic expression, anguish over child pornography and fear of new technology have converged to make this a particularly dangerous time for sexually explicit expression in this country. In fact, anxiety over sexual expression has reached such heights that the president has just signed into law the Communications Decency Act, a measure that will criminalise not just obscenity but even profane language when publicly transmitted in cyberspace.

The artists most in danger right now, politically and legally, are those who work with the most taboo of subjects — childhood sexuality. Such artists are working at a time when the problem of child pornography has taken centre stage in our political debate. As Congress rushes to pass new laws to combat the problem, the federal courts, disquieted by the dangers of child sexual abuse, have tolerated laws that define child pornography in increasingly broad and subjective terms. Their concern about the threat to children has led the Supreme Court to reject in their child pornography cases some of the most important speech-protective features of the law of adult obscenity. One casualty has been the traditional protection afforded to artistic expression.

It has long been a principle of adult obscenity law that no matter how shocking or how offensive a sexually explicit work might otherwise be, it is protected speech if it demonstrates serious artistic value. (Unfortunately, this principle doesn't always seem so clear in practice — consider, for example, the obscenity prosecution brought against a museum and its director for displaying the works of Robert Mapplethorpe).

But under the more restrictive law of child pornography, the question of whether or not a work is art has become irrelevant. Because child pornography laws are premised on the notion that material must be suppressed because of harm done to the actual children pictured, the Court has so far refused to draw an exception to these laws for works that possess serious artistic value. As the Court reasoned in its first child pornography ruling in 1982, 'It is irrelevant to the child [who has been abused] whether or not the material...has [artistic] value.' In a later case, Justice Brennan warned the court of the threat the new laws posed to the tradition of great artists — from Donatello to Degas — who have portrayed child nudity. But his concerns fell on deaf ears, as an uneasy Court created a rule of law that would have a chilling effect on artistic expression.

What makes the child pornography cases more dangerous for artists is that the Court has upheld laws that define child pornography in extremely vague and broad terms. In *Osborne v Ohio*, the Court held constitutional a statute prohibiting child nudity if there was a 'graphic focus on the genitals'. Recently, a federal Court of Appeals chose an interpretation of the federal child pornography laws so expansive — it could apply to exhibition of genital areas even if they are covered by clothing — that even the US solicitor general initially thought it went too far.

Some artists have already paid a price: Jock Sturges' studio was ransacked by the FBI; an art student in New Jersey was taken away from his family for several months last year because he photographed his nude five-year-old daughter for a class assignment. (A psychologist later testified that the only harm suffered by the child was from having been subjected to police interrogation and from having had her father removed from her family.) Recently, a prosecution was brought (then dropped on technical grounds) against a bookstore for selling Pasolini's film *Salo* — a graphic, harrowing, yet highly acclaimed film showing fascists' sexual torture of children.

Other artists have so far escaped prosecution, but appear extremely vulnerable under the law — Sally Mann, for example, who takes nude photographs of her children that some people view as erotic. Consider the

HOUK FRIEDMAN, NEW YORK

SALLY MANN Virginia at 6 *1991*

BARBARA GLADSTONE GALLERY, NEW YORK

RICHARD PRINCE Brooke Shields (Spiritual America) *1983, ektacolour print 24x20"*

photographs of Larry Clark, who in his book *Teenage Lust*, captured minors engaged in explicit, sometimes violent sexual conduct. (One of his pictures documents the apparent rape of a young girl while she was on hallucinogenic drugs.)

Mann and Clark work in a legal no-man's zone. I am convinced that I could be arrested in some states for showing Larry Clark's pictures, even in a lecture. Some of his work appears so clearly violative of existing child pornography laws that the only thing that could save him if he were prosecuted would be an exception for work of artistic value, an exception the Court has so far refused to draw.

It is no accident that these artists are photographers, because photography is the medium most vulnerable right now to prosecution. It is only when a real child is involved that child pornography law becomes the rubric under which a work is judged.

What is so disturbing about photography? One answer is that there is an exploitation inherent in photographs; they capture your soul; they trick you about the real. As Susan Sontag tells us in *On Photography*:

> To photograph people is to violate them, by seeing them as they never see themselves, by having knowledge of them they can never have; it turns people into objects that can be symbolically possessed... [T]o photograph someone is a sublimated murder...

Sally Mann's work exploits this quality. Is she taking advantage of her children's sexuality for her own work? One critic pitied her 'helpless art-abused children', sometimes pictured in scenarios where they appear injured, raising questions about Mann's maternal nature. The possibility of exploitation and abuse in Mann's work comments on the betrayal and violence inherent in photography.

It is not only photography's capacity to betray and capture a subject that disturbs us. It is also photography's heightened sense of the real; it confounds us as viewers, tempting us to mistake representation for reality, to see abuse itself rather than pictures that raise questions about abuse. Again, Mann's pictures draw on this disturbing power of the medium. In a picture called *Damaged Child*, Mann's daughter's face appears swollen and injured, implying that she has been battered; in fact, Mann took the picture after her daughter got a mere bug bite.

Another danger for photography is that its close alliance with reality has led to its historical devaluation — its second-class status as an art form. There is a sense with photography that 'anyone can do it,' as if photographers were not 'serious' artists. This persistent suspicion that photography is not 'real art' suggests that even if the court were to create an exception for serious artistic value under the child pornography laws, as it has done for obscenity laws, it might not suffice to protect artists like Sally Mann, who work in a medium that is already suspect.

Finally, the vulnerability of photography to censorship may reflect our deeply rooted cultural anxieties about the image. There is a strain of élitism in this anxiety. Traditionally images have been the books of the illiterate;

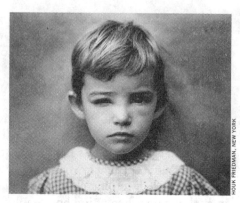

SALLY MANN Damaged Child *1984*

stained-glass windows told the stories of the Bible to those who couldn't read it. The history of censorship is to some extent the history of suppressing and controlling what people see, based on elitist fears of mass access. Anyone who censors is putting himself in a position of condescension. He's saying, 'I can look at this image in a cool, dispassionate way, but I must protect those people weaker than me. They may be vulnerable to the image. It may incite them to rape or violence or madness.'

Ironically, at the same time that Larry Clark and Sally Mann are so vulnerable to censorship, it is essential to note their commercial and critical success: Mann's shows sell out; Larry Clark has been embraced by the film industry — his first film, *Kids*, was a critical success last summer. Mann's and Clark's success, coupled with their legal vulnerability, suggests the complex relationship between legal taboo and artistic expression, a relationship echoed in other areas of our culture. Last summer at the height of media and political anguish over child pornography, Calvin Klein introduced his notorious and wildly successful jeans advertisements that looked like the fetish photographs of a paedophile.

Sometimes culture responds to the law as if it were a dare. Perhaps the new censoriousness in America has invited the very cultural expression it seeks to repress. ❏

Amy Adler is a New York-based attorney who writes frequently about art censorship issues. She will be joining the faculty of New York University Law School this autumn

EDWARD LUCIE-SMITH

Megaphones for the dispossessed

'An awful lot of what was introduced in a kind of anti-establishment spirit has — such is the irony of things — found its way into the highest precincts of contemporary high art, as if co-operation were irresistible, and the art world, like the commercial world, feeds and flourishes on what was intended to call it in question and overthrow it.' Arthur C Danto in 'Bad Aesthetic Times' from Encounters and Reflections: Art in the Historical Present, *(Farrar, Straus & Giroux, New York, 1990)*

WHY have museums and other 'official' exhibition venues become the places, above all others, where minority groupings, or groupings which see themselves as in some way disadvantaged, seek to assert their cultural rights? The phenomenon attracted widespread attention thanks to the so-called 'politically correct' Whitney Biennial of 1993, an exhibition which ranged widely over issues of gender as well as those of race. This attention was reinforced by the publication in the same year of Robert Hughes's polemical book, *Culture of Complaint*. Essentially, however, what was happening was not new. Its roots can be traced to a number of sources, some located a long way back in the history of Modernism.

There was, for example, the long drawn out struggle to create a separate and recognisable African American art. This began in the mid-1920s — the key date was 1925 when Alain Locke published his influential essay 'The Legacy of the Ancestral Arts'. Locke, a Harvard-educated philosopher who became a professor at Howard University, was a prominent representative of a new generation of black middle-class intellectuals. Seeking cultural legitimisation for blacks, now migrating in large numbers from the rural poverty-stricken south to the industrial cities of the north, Howard wanted African Americans to reclaim the great heritage of African art. The paradox was that the way in which both he

BENNY ANDREWS Flora *1969, oil and collage, 50x42cm*

and others like him regarded this art was strongly coloured by the use which early (white) modernists had already made of it. The Africanising art produced by painters such as Lois Mailou Jones, an African American painter of the interwar years who spent a substantial period in Paris, was influenced directly by such things as African masks, but perhaps even more by Picasso's *Demoiselles d'Avignon.*

The Civil Rights Movement of the 1960s and 1970s inevitably found an echo in American museums, which tend to reflect the more liberal and experimental aspects of American culture. The 1970s, in particular, saw important exhibitions devoted to African American art, such as 'Jubilee: Afro-American Artists in Afro America', staged at the Museum of Fine Arts Boston in 1975, and 'Two Centuries of Black American Art' at the Los Angeles County Museum the following year. Writers about African American art increasingly tended to strike a much more militant, and indeed separatist, note. The following comes from a book published in 1970:

> Black art is a didactic art form rising from a strong nationalistic base and characterised by its commitment to a) use of the past and its heroes to inspire heroic and revolutionary ideas, b) to use recent political and social events to teach recognition, control and extermination of 'the enemy', and c) to project the future which the nation can expect after the struggle is won.[1]

Much African American art of the period — the work of Benny Andrews, David Hammons and Betye Saar for example — was aggressively political in response to the spirit of the period.

It is a mistake, however, to view the development of a fiercely political African American art as an event which took place in isolation. To the superficial observer, the art of the 1970s, like that of the second half of the 1960s, was dominated by tendencies which seemed to insist that art was a totally separate realm. This was especially the case in America (which continued to monopolise the attention of most commentators on contemporary art). For the critics, key events were exhibitions such as 'Primary Structures' at the Jewish Museum, New York, in 1966; 'Anti-Illusion: Procedures/Materials', at the Whitney in 1969; 'Conceptual Art and Conceptual Aspects' at the New York Cultural Center in 1970, and 'Art about Art', once again at the Whitney, in 1978.

These much discussed shows distracted attention from other, equally significant phenomena. One was the rise of feminist art, signalled by the setting up of the first feminist art course, organised by Judy Chicago, at Pomona College in California in 1971, and by the survey exhibition 'Women Painters, 1550-1950' presented at the Los Angeles County Museum in 1976. In Germany, meanwhile, art was taking an entirely different direction from that which it seemed to be pursuing in the USA. The German political situation, and in particular the division of the country into East and West, prompted the creation of art in which political issues were central. An early indicator of what was happening was the

'Kunst und Politik' show at Wuppertal in 1970. Most significant of all, however, was the rise to prominence of Joseph Beuys.

Beuys totally changed perceptions about art and what it could do. Beginning as a fringe figure in the neo-Dadaist Fluxus Group, German-based but dominated by Americans, and by avant-garde musicians rather than by artists, Beuys took the 'happenings' already popularised by the Pop artists in America and transformed them into what he called 'actions'. The difference in the nature of the two terms is significant. A happening implies something passive, in the sense that it is without long-term consequences. The event occurs, then dissolves again and vanishes. Beuys's alternative label carries with it a subliminal message that what is done is designed in some way or other to change the world. In the 1970s, Beuys became more and more involved with politics, which he redefined as 'social sculpture'. In 1971 he founded the Organisation for Direct Democracy Through Referendum. At 'Documenta 5', held in Kassel in 1972, he conducted 100 days of debate with the international public who visited the show, and the room where he held forth was easily the most heavily frequented section of the whole display. He repeated the exercise at 'Documenta 6' in 1977, as part of what he now called his Free University for Creativity and Interdisciplinary Research.

The Kassel Documenta exhibitions were at the height of their influence in the 1970s, as the most ambitious surveys of the avant-garde art of their day, and Beuys's success with the public they attracted made him the most celebrated member of a new German avant-garde, now starting to assert itself as an alternative to the American domination of contemporary art which had established itself with the rise of Abstract Expressionism in the mid-1940s. Paradoxically, he left the American avant-garde establishment suspicious and a little at a loss. There was a comic incident during his first visit to New York in 1973, when he asked to meet the leading figures in the new feminist art movement. The women came, but they were suspicious of his motives, and some found him condescending. When he asked the gathering what he could do for them, the African American artist Faith Ringgold replied loudly: 'Get behind us and push!' Beuys was not to have a major American retrospective until 1979, when he was taken on, with some misgivings, by the Guggenheim Museum. Before this, only a very small part of the American exhibition-going public had been in contact with his art.

Beuys's relationship to the new 'issue-based' art which arose in the

USA is therefore an oblique one. There are, nevertheless, several features of it which are worth pondering. Beuys's career offers parallels with those of certain saints and prophetesses of the late Middle Ages — specifically Joan of Arc (Beuys himself aimed higher — there are a number of autobiographical artworks which draw a parallel between himself and Jesus Christ[2]). Joan was an individual who came from nowhere, and arrogated to herself the right to tell kings and other politically powerful people what to do. Her authority for doing so was her 'voices' — in other words her conviction that she was a chosen vehicle for divine commands. Since the time of the Romantic Movement, artists have increasingly tended to see themselves, not as essentially makers of objects, but as chosen vessels. There were already traces of this in the second phase of Minimal art, as this developed in the late 1960s. See, for example, this statement, made by the leading Minimal sculptor Robert Morris, printed in the April 1969 issue of the avant-garde art magazine *Artforum*:

> Under attack is the rationalistic notion that art is a form of work that results in a finished product... what art now has in its hands is mutable stuff which need not arrive at the point of being finalized with respect to either time or space. The notion that work is an irreversible process ending in a static icon-object no longer has much relevance.[3]

Morris's work, like that of other critically acclaimed American avant-gardists of the same generation, such as Richard Serra and Bruce Nauman (generally regarded as Beuys's closest disciple in the USA), nevertheless remained within a closed aesthetic world. What was needed was an opening to the universe outside the museum, of the kind Beuys was already attempting to make in Germany. This came about through the political upheavals which shook America in the 1970s. It no longer seemed acceptable that artists should remain isolated from the general turmoil.

Basically, the new politically based art came from two quite different directions. There was work which asserted the identity — also, often, the radical separateness within American society — not only of African Americans, but of other ethnic groupings, chiefly in this case Hispanic. There was also work based on sexuality and gender. The Hispanic initiatives, newer and more direct than their African American counterparts, are in some ways more informative. The most discussed was the Chicano art movement in Los Angeles. Chicanos are Americans of

Mexican descent, though by no means all Mexican Americans accept the designation. Chicano art arose in the 1970s as a popular, untutored phenomenon. Perhaps the best-known examples of this phase are the murals at the Estrada Courts Housing Project in East Los Angeles, which date from the mid- to late-1970s. The murals show a wide variety of influences — the work of Diego Rivera and other Mexican muralists of the 1930s and 1940s, popular wall paintings in Mexican cantinas, religious oleographs in Mexican calendars. One of the main influences, however, was not Mexican at all. It was Cuban revolutionary posters, made available through a large-format popular book, *The Art of Revolution, 1959-70*, published in 1971 with an introduction by the East Coast intellectual Susan Sontag.

Like the graffiti art which manifested itself in New York at the same period, Chicano painting eventually moved from the great outdoors into commercial art galleries and finally into museums. The first step was the show 'Chicanismo en el arte', mounted by the Los Angeles County Museum in 1975. The most comprehensive survey so far was 'CARA — Chicano Art, Resistance and Affirmation', held at the Wight Gallery, University of California, Los Angeles, in 1991. By this time, however, Chicano art was already well established as one of a whole range of similar manifestations, comprehensively chronicled in an influential book by the leading feminist critic and art historian, Lucy Lippard, *Mixed Blessings: Art in a Multicultural America* (Abrams, New York 1990).

Ethnically based art is, however, a curiously uneven manifestation, even in the USA, where it has won most visibility. For example, the Cuban community in Florida, though apparently just as coherent culturally, has not come together artistically in the same fashion as the Chicanos. The one major survey of art by Cuban expatriates living in the USA, 'Outside Cuba: Fuera da Cuba', a touring exhibition mounted in 1989 by the combined forces of the University of Miami, Florida, and Rutgers State University, New Jersey, revealed that the artists concerned were essentially eclectic modernists and postmodernists, with no cohesive cultural force to bind them together. The influence of Cuban revolutionary posters, perhaps understandably, was nowhere to be seen, and allusions to popular culture, Cuban or from the colony of Cuban exiles in Miami, were very few.

The other moving force in the new political art was feminism. Whereas minority, ethnically based art usually, though not invariably, had

JOSEPH BEUYS Aus Berlin: Neues Vom Kojoten *1979, sculptural environment including felt blanket, gloves, walking stick, flashlight, chime, hay,* Wall Street Journal, *hat, coyote hair, plaster rubble, acetylene lanterns on sticks, arc light, sulphur*

its roots among people living near the bottom of the class and economic structure, and moved into the museum sphere through the patronage of mediators who did not belong to the original group, this was not the case with feminist art, which, like feminism in general, is usually a middle-class phenomenon and the product not only of strong and extremely determined personalities, but also of artists who are well educated and *au courant* with everything that had happened under Modernism. Indeed, if one wants to identify a single factor in the triumph of the new political art it must be the success of feminist theory in the USA, and specifically its impact on art criticism, combined with a feminist conquest of curatorial posts in leading museums, and of equivalent editorial posts in the leading publishing houses which produce art books.

The conquest was by no means immediate, despite the gains feminist art made in the 1970s. To begin with, feminist art faced entrenched hostility in the museum community, of a kind African American manifestations (for example) had long overcome. Judy Chicago, in a recently published book of memoirs, *Beyond the Flower* (Viking, New York 1996) recalls the initial difficulties in getting further museum showings for her ambitious installation *The Dinner Party*, certainly the key feminist artwork of its period, despite the immense success of the premier exhibition at the San Francisco Museum of Modern Art in 1979. She also has something to say about the general significance of the piece:

> Historically, women have either been excluded from the process of creating the definitions of what is considered art or allowed to participate only if we accept and work within existing mainstream designations. If women have no real role as women in the process of defining art, then we are essentially prevented from helping to shape the cultural symbols. In part, *The Dinner Party* was intended to test whether a woman artist, working in monumental scale and with a level of ambition usually reserved for men, could count on the art system to support art with female content.[4]

There are a number of important assumptions here. First — as is indeed self-evident — that feminist art has content which goes well beyond the aesthetic. Second, that it has to seek for new forms to express this content. Third, that one of its primary functions is propagandistic. That is, it takes over the museum in order to try and turn the system against itself, since one of the chief symbolic functions of the museum-as-institution is to present the cultural establishment in fully concrete and visible form.

From its beginnings, feminist art favoured forms which did not carry a 'patriarchal' taint. It was wary of what was object-based. It preferred installations, performances, videos. In this sense it fitted in with what was already happening in art, as can be seen from the declaration by Robert Morris already quoted. What had been simply the latest in a long series of aesthetic initiatives, dating back to the very beginning of the Modern Movement, was seized upon by feminist theorists (themselves much influenced by French deconstructionists such as Jacques Derrida). Beuys, though he wanted to change society, wanted to do so as a single charismatic individual, fulfilling role models inherited not only from medieval sainthood but also from a nearer source: the vision of the artist as an embattled outcast-hero inherited from the Romantic Movement. Feminist art, by contrast, was a consciously collective effort. Its aim was not merely to alter the existing social situation, treating it, in Beuysian terms, as material for 'social sculpture', but to de-construct it altogether: to take it apart and put it together in a new way. The minority art forms — primarily African American and Chicano in the USA, and Afro-Caribbean in Britain — were never quite so ambitious, though glad enough to participate when institutional doors were thrown open to them.

The result, in the 1990s, has been the curious situation outlined in the quotation from the American art-critic and philosopher Arthur C Danto at the head of this essay. Museums of contemporary art, particularly in the USA, have become strongholds of the 'politically correct' opposition to the conservative tendencies now seen in other, more traditional forms of political activity. In addition, because of the continuing prestige of American art, this political correctness has been paraded even in situations where it is not particularly relevant. Dutch museums, for example, are more interested in African American or even British Afro-Caribbean art than they are in the products of their local Surinamese or Javanese communities. In 1989, as the latest American novelty, Chicano art received a major showing in Nantes, France[5], where few Chicanos can have been seen in person. That is, protest is in some danger of becoming a universal museum language, even in situations where people are no longer quite sure what is being protested about.

There are other potential disadvantages as well. The emphasis on political correctness leads directly to two things. First, a kind of forced egalitarianism, a quota system, especially for large mixed exhibitions, where an artist is included, not for his or her merits, but because he or she represents a particular disadvantaged group. This attitude was particularly marked in the Whitney Biennial of 1993, already mentioned, but has since receded a little. Second, an indifference to the visual qualities of the artwork, so long as its author comes from the right background and its actual content toes the expected line. Rarely can museums of contemporary art have featured so many things which are truly dismal to look at, in the name of helping lame dogs over styles.

The main drawback of the present situation is, however, not in the museums themselves but in art education. Because so much 'politically correct' art is not object-oriented, it will leave surprisingly little trace behind it in the permanent collections of the institutions which now shelter it. In a real sense, therefore, it will pass from museum memory. The more lasting consequence is likely to be elsewhere. The spate of museum shows devoted to polemical art offered during the past decade has sanctioned a new attitude not only towards what art is taught, but how art is taught. This is particularly the case in America, where the most recent art falls into the educational net (as it generally doesn't in Britain).

Whitney Museum of American Art 1993 Biennial Exhibition (left to right)
CINDY SHERMAN, *Untitled 1992*, ALISON SAAR *Hi Yella, 1991*, CINDY SHERMAN, *Untitled, 1992*, CINDY SHERMAN, *Untitled, 1992*

As an author of books on contemporary art who occasionally ventures into the educational field, I have in the last few years been subjected to transatlantic editorial pressures of a type previously unknown to me. The pressure starts when the synopsis is first submitted, and a count is made of the number of female artists I intend to include (the question posed is not 'are there enough?' but 'are there more than in any other work which might be considered a direct competitor?'). It continues even when the text is already very late in going to the printer, with a list of additional artists, mostly ethnic and/or female, whom I must include in my final chapters, 'because these are the names our people expect to teach'. The attraction of those included in the list seems to be, in almost every case, that the artist concerned is pushing a very crude, very simple racial or feminist message. Untrammelled, as it happens, by aesthetics — which must make teaching them a lot easier.

Reverting to Victorian attitudes, the American educational system increasingly values art not for its own sake but as a purveyor of moral messages. At this point the radicals within the museum system and the conservatives outside it shake hands with one another. ❏

Edward Lucie-Smith *is a well-known UK writer and broadcaster on art. His most recent book is* ArToday *(Phaidon 1996).* Movements in art since 1945: issues and concepts *was reissued last year by Thames and Hudson in their World of Art series*

1 Edmund Barry Gaither, *Afro-American Artists, New York and Boston* (Boston: The National Center of Afro-American Artists, 1970), pp3-4
2 For example, *Arena*, first shown in Naples in 1982, and now in the collection of the Dia Foundation, New York — see Lynne Cooke, *Joseph Beuys: Arena — where would I have got if I had been intelligent!* (Dia Center for the Arts, New York, 1994)
3 Reprinted in the catalogue of *The New Sculpture 1965-1975*, edited by Richard Armstrong and Richard Marshall (Whitney Museum, New York, 1990), p185
4 Judy Chicago, *Beyond the Flower: The Autobiography of a Feminist Artist*, (Viking, New York 1996), pp71-2
5 See the catalogue, *Le Demon des Anges: 16 artistes chicanos autour de Los Angeles* (Centre de Recherche pour le développement culturel, Nantes, 1989)

JUDY CHICAGO

JUDY CHICAGO The Dinner Party *1979, mixed media; 48x48x48'*

Welcome to dinner

' A N immense open table covered with fine white cloths is set with
thirty-nine place settings, thirteen on a side, each commemorating
a goddess, historic personage, or important woman. Though most are
largely unknown, their names should be as familiar to us as the male heroes
whose exploits we absorb from childhood through art, myth, literature,
history, and popular entertainment. *The Dinner Party* suggests that these
female heroes are equally worthy of commemoration, as are those
hundreds of others whose names are inscribed upon the *Heritage Floor...*

'OVER the years, many people have asked me why the museums refused to show *The Dinner Party*. I have tried to explain that neither financial nor popular success necessarily guarantee museum support. Moreover, the negative institutional response to *The Dinner Party* seemed to be part of a larger pattern of discrimination against women and women's art... With the exception of Lucy Lippard, writing in *Art in America*, and John Perrault, in the now-defunct *Soho News*, the New York art establishment rained down a barrage of hostile criticisms and virulent misrepresentations of the piece in such publications as *The New York Times, Time* magazine, and *The New York Review of Books*. One influential reviewer deemed it grotesque "kitsch," but a more destructive remark, which set the tone for a considerable amount of subsequent writing, was that *The Dinner Party* could be best described as little more than vaginas on plates.

'THE DINNER PARTY was discussed [on 26 July 1990] as part of the debate on [University of the District of Columbia's] budget, which Congress controls. Then-representative Stan Parris from Virginia introduced an amendment that would delete $1.6 million from the school's operating budget, "in direct response to...[the] offensiveness to the sensitivities and moral values of our various related communities." He went on to ask, "What kinds of art...what value system are we, the Federal lawmakers, responsible for promoting in this, the nation's Capital, by being asked to give our imprimatur of approval to this particular work?"

Parris argued for his amendment on the grounds of fiscal impropriety, which was entirely inaccurate. Nonetheless, he managed to convince a number of liberal congressmen — including my own representative, the usually astute Bill Richardson — to support his measure. But there was another and ultimately more distressing accusation about *The Dinner Party*, first put forth by Robert Dornan of California and then amplified by his colleague Dana Rohrbacher, who came right out and said that *The Dinner Party* was "pornographic," which is what Parris's comments about "offensiveness" probably implied.

"We now have this pornographic art," railed Dornan, "I mean, three-dimensional ceramic art of 39 women's vaginal areas, their genitalia, served up on plates." After introducing the *Washington Times's* distorted reports directly into the Congressional Record, the congressman went on to make the entirely fictional statement that the piece had been "banned in art galleries around the country...and characterized as obscene."

Several congressmen (no women participated in the debate) attempted to counter these charges, notably Ron Dellums (also of California) and Pat Williams of Montana, but to no avail. The Parris Amendment was passed by a large majority and the university was left to deal with this reduced budget.

During the summer of 1990, the Christian Television Network picked up on the UDC/*Dinner Party* controversy, with the Reverend Pat Robertson apparently blasting the art on his *700 Club* show. It was reported to me that the black religious right had actually circulated rumors that the reason *The Dinner Party* was in storage was that the crates contained the Devil and that I was the Antichrist. Even the normally liberal columnist Mary McGrory got into the act. With a seeming lack of journalistic responsibility, she wrote about *The Dinner Party*, reportedly without having ever seen it, repeating the nonsense that it was "obscene."...It seemed as though *The Dinner Party* had been deliberately misrepresented in both the art community and in Congress, promulgating an image of it that bore little resemblance to the piece's goal of teaching women's history through art and honoring our aesthetic, intellectual, and philosophical achievements.

The right wing, for all its foolishness, has the uncanny ability to discern that the opening up of the symbol system — particularly visual art — to the voices and experiences of women, people of color, gays and lesbians, and other marginalized groups challenges the control of representation upon which the prevailing value system rests...' ❏

• *The Dinner Party* **had its first public presentation at the San Francisco Museum of Modern Art in 1979. During the following decade, *The Dinner Party* was seen in 14 institutions in six different countries. From 24 April-18 August, it will be the focal point of a new exhibition at the University College of Los Angeles Armand Hammer Museum of Modern Art. The exhibition presents a broad history of feminist art from the 1960s to the 1990s under the title 'Sexual Politics: Judy Chicago's *Dinner Party* in Feminist Art History'. The exhibition will be accompanied by a fully illustrated catalogue with essays by feminist scholars and critics, from which these excerpts are taken**

© Judy Chicago *The Dinner Party* (Viking Penguin USA, March 1996)

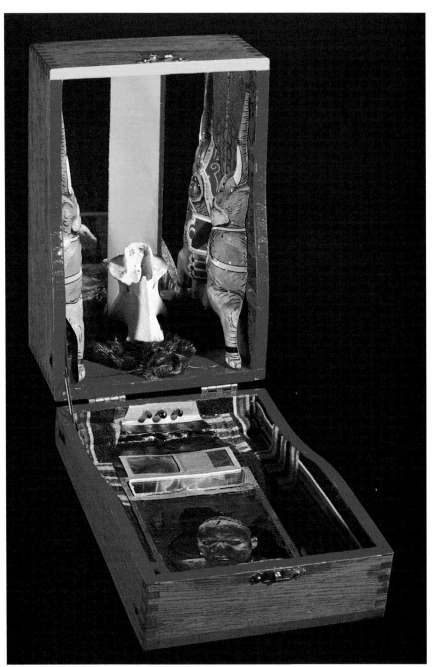

BETYE SAAR Africa *1968 (Private Collection/Visual Arts Library, London)*

SAM GILLIAM Half Pint of Whisky/Clarinet *1990, acrylic on sculpted canvas, acrylic and enamel on aluminium 58x48x22" (Private Collection/Visual Arts Library, London)*

JOSEPH BEUYS Self-portrait *1972, silkscreen/acetate 190x102cm*
(Private Collection/Visual Arts Library, London ©DACS 1996)

ANON Mural, USA California, 1984
(Photo ©Edward Lucie-Smith/Visual Arts Library, London)

JUDY CHICAGO Placesetting: Caroline Herschel from The Dinner Party *1979, mixed media, plate 14" diameter (Photo ©Donald Woodman/Through the Flower)*

KEITH PIPER Another Step into the Arena *1992, 4 monitor, 3 source video installation with mixed video projection. Installation: 'front' (Het Kijkhuis, The Hague, Holland) (Courtesy the artist / Visual Arts Library, London)*

RICHARD PRINCE All You Can Eat *1996, acrylic and silkscreen on canvas 84x96"*
(Saatchi Collection, London, 1996)

TONY OURSLER Good/Bad *1995, mixed media, video projection, dimensions variable*
(Saatchi Collection, London, 1996)

OKWUI ENWEZOR

Writing inside the hyphen

The work of African American artist Carrie Mae Weems confronts the world and its bad faith towards repressed groups: those whose every gesture towards speech has been hounded and terrorised into muteness

WHEN recalling certain histories of violence and their effacement of collective memory as a critical basis for making art, is there a better way to rebuke Theodor Adorno on his tacit acquiescence to mechanisms of this effacement than to start with the slave narrative? Adorno once wrote that after Auschwitz, writing poetry was not possible. Heard through and spoken within earshot of the great poetry of Paul Celan, who survived one such camp, which Adorno marked as the edge where memory fails, one cannot help thinking how thoroughly incorrect the philosopher was then, and remains today.

In many ways, African Americans in their quest for a share in the idea of Americanness must also feel the compulsion to lapse into Adorno's perpetual silence; the urge to still the tide of memories that flow out of the violent experience of slavery. For to be American is to disavow any claim to origin, to erase the past and its seams. However, the quest to lay claim to this accursed share suffers a temporal and spatial disruption in the location of the hyphen, in the hybrid space which must be accounted for in order to transcend territorialisation on the margins.

In matters of memory, the slave narrative is a counter-memory. It is deeply rooted in a structure of signification that refuses closure, and in many ways seeks to recover and reclaim that which lies outside the sentence. The slave narrative is the quintessential journey of self-affirmation. It is a testimony to the arduous battle to claim a voice, to speak on one's own behalf, to dislocate the classical enlightenment episteme of the ahistorical African subject. The slave narrative presages the transgressive, counter-hegemonic prosody of much postmodern art, upon whose radical and critical edge African American artists like Carrie Mae Weems stand.

Without foreclosing its broader concern with questions of representation, and how those questions play on the fields of aesthetics, philosophy and politics, Carrie Mae Weems' work takes its precedence from the structure of the slave narrative, and finds it inspiration in the work of Toni Morrison.

Weems creates her work in series. Each series represents both a denotative and connotative aspect of signification, propelled and threaded through a complex of social taboos, icons, and conceptual frameworks that refer to the active and inert historicity of African Americans as subjects. In the series 'Environmental Portraits', which she began early in her career in 1978 in her hometown, Portland, Oregon, and later continued in places like New York, Mexico, Southern California, and Fiji, Weems' emphasis was on addressing and portraying the subject in his/her own space. By photographing people in their natural surroundings, her aim was not only to extricate them from confinement in the space of the dissimilar, but, in a way, to territorialise them outside the space of ambivalence and abjection.

However, it is in Weems' next series, 'Family Pictures and Stories' (1981-82), that truly challenging elements of her work began to emerge. Still working within documentary practice, she began to employ text in which the first person account of the text appears more spoken than written. What emerges from this series is how this simple transition from straight photography to her embedding of narrative within its presentation, allows Weems to bridge the distance from detached observer of social environments to subject within the stories' narratives. In turn, she is able to reposition and interrogate notions of photographic representation as objective truth teller, as a means to arrest and record complex issues of identity.

Beginning with the series 'Ain't Joking' (1987-88), the work became more experimental, her approach more psychologically complex. The series, explains Weems, 'deals exclusively with the stereotyping of Afro-Americans by whites,' as part of the continuing saga of their difficult political and social situation within American history. Images with titles

IN 1944 MY FATHER WENT TO WAR.
PULLED A TRIGGER,
SHOT A NIGGER,
THAT WAS THE END OF THE WAR.

CARRIE MAE WEEMS A Child's Verse 'In 1944 my father went to war' *1987, silver print, 14.5x14.5"*

like *Black Woman with Chicken*, which shows a young African American woman holding a chicken drum stick, are staged with props that play with racial stereotypes, myths, and fictions of black identity, in which the props signify the hidden meaning of the stereotype. *What are three things you can't give a black person?* to which the answer is 'A black eye, a fat lip, and a job', addresses the dire and embattled state of black masculinity, while *Mirror, Mirror*, speaks to the unappreciation of black feminine beauty and its supposed inferiority to white femininity. In each of these instances

Weems' mode of address is directed at the injurious nature of misrepresentation and its violent legacy on the lives of black people.

Nowhere is this more clearly articulated in the series than in the photograph: *A Child's Verse (In 1944 my father went to war)* which uses an appropriated image of grinning white supremacists, under which the verse is printed: 'In 1944 my father went to war/pulled a trigger/shot a nigger/that was the end of the war.' Buttressed by language in such a complex *pas des deux* of signification, the photographs in this series explore America's continuing obsession with race, and how those obsessions come to unsettle and devalue the coherence, worth and self-image of African Americans socially, culturally and politically. Yet in employing these props, it seems that Weems was not only aiming to ironise their sting but, equally, to disarm and delimit their oppressive effects.

What, however, caught my interest in Weems' oeuvre is the manner in which she has co-opted and turned over the historical archive as the source of the hidden meanings of what binds America to its submerged past. Weems' purposeful rearrangement of the archive has taken a wide dimension in recent years. Rummaging through its dusty cupboards and forgotten alcoves she unearths popular icons of blacks as minstrels, images of lynchings and brutal beatings, social taboos related to miscegenation and black sexuality which continue to play on the imagination of the American mainstream, and are given force through the marginalising imperatives and coordinates of the mass media. In the series 'American Icons' (1988-89), Weems photographed ceramic wares of minstrels and mammies popularised in the early and middle part of this century as sources of entertainment and replicated in the cinema of the period. With their exaggerated eyes and huge lips, these despicable icons of American racism and violence against African Americans are used to reinforce within viewers their own complicity in framing the efficacy of these icons as objective stand-ins for the deformed black body. In Weems' work the injury of such images is incalculable. And the manner in which she sets them up as still lifes in a diorama, recasts them in an ethnographic framework. Thus our attention is further directed to ethnography's complicity in creating a defamiliarising effect of the African American as a sub human species which exists somewhere between the ape and human.

In *And 22 Million Very Tired and Very Angry People* (1991), Weems also deploys totems and iconic symbols of black resistance; employing them to speak about the resilience of African American survival, its popular memory, and its will to fight persecution and subjugation. In *Untitled* (Sea Islands Series 1991-92), it is the memory of Africa and the survival of its mores and folklore that Weems packs into her novelistic narratives.

Carrie Mae Weems is the quintessential American artist: for the past two decades her work has engaged, interrogated, and poeticised the sweep of American history in both its grandeur and squalor. Her work lays claim to a tradition in which the presence of African America is darkly illumined and given force of character as the central core of what defines American life and culture, as a window through which America looks out to face the world. Throughout its formation, American history has subsisted on the negation and presence, repulsion and desire, marking and erasing of powerful vestiges both of its native cultures and the captive cultures that defined it. Blind to their own prejudices and bad faith, prominent art critics and historians recreate this paradox by representing the art of African American artists outside the critical interpretation of American culture.

Yet it could be said that Weems' range of topics, in which she delves into the enclosures occupied by narratives of race, gender, class and sexuality, is more than the sum of American historical traditions. On a much larger scale, her work confronts the world and its monumental bad faith towards repressed groups; those whose every gesture towards speech has been historically terrorised and hounded into muteness, effecting the kind of erasure that creates the misimpression of African American subjectivity as a void, and often turning its eloquent portents into syntactical chaos.

The writings of Toni Morrison, the Nobel laureate, whose critical interrogation of the American literary canon in her book *Playing in the Dark* posited this void as what distinguishes American literature, based as it is on the shadow of the black subject. Remarking on this shadow, Morrison writes of how 'certain absences are so stressed they arrest us with their intentionality and purpose, like neighbourhoods that are defined by the population held away from them.' By evoking this history so explicitly one could say that Carrie Mae Weems has not only reclaimed that neighbourhood, but has reterritorialised it. ❑

Okwui Enwezor *is the editor/publisher of* Nka: Journal of Contemporary African Art. *He is the co-curator of* In/Sight: African Photographers, 1940-Present *on view at the Guggenheim Museum in New York from May-September 1996. He lives in New York*

Young Americans

A rt is what society decrees to be art and it is those artists who hold up the mirror to this *fin de siècle* American society who are most often in the critical firing line. Much, though not all, of the new art in the USA is issues-based, the expression of such 'minority' concerns as race, sex, gender, cultural identity. Its images are designed to shock, disturb, confound and define the society they confront.

GREGORY GREEN Suitcase Bomb #9 (NY)
mixed media, 17x19x21'

Given the prominence of this art in public museums and galleries, it can no longer be relegated to the margins reserved for minorities; no more ignored than the reflection of rage and frustration at the heart of America in the mirror held up to mainstream society by its young artists.

'Young Americans: New American Art in the Saatchi Collection' offers a bleak, uncompromising vision. Decay and detritus, paranoia and despair compete with nostalgia for those mythical nineteenth-century traditional values. For the golden age of lost suburban innocence when 'every small American town had its big red fire truck' (à la Charles Ray's *Fire Truck*, 1993) lovingly maintained by volunteers', against the new suburban culture of men 'seething in silent anger at bureaucratic government, powerful business interests and various real and imagined enemies' that lies behind Gregory Green's installations *Nuclear Device #2* or *Work Station #5,* and encapsulates post-Oklahoma revelations of 'weapons stockpiled in preparation for house-to-house combat and radio equipment ready for emergency broadcast'.

The paranoia that consumes America's angry men in militia uniforms is echoed again in Tony Oursler's images/projections of equally disturbed — though probably better-educated — Americans: hysteria, schizophrenia, a passive, lobotomised audience, angry victims of a mindless media culture. This, it seems, is the American condition. As is the aura of defeat and hopeless that clings to the last hope saloons and lost bars of Richard Prince's abstractions.

Art is criticism of life said someone. Or is it life that has overcome art with its messages of a society not 'sick at the extremities' but disintegrating from within.

Tony Oursler: true or false

'ENCOUNTERING one of Oursler's figures is like being startled by a schizophrenic who thrusts himself at you on a New York street. Even a hardened New Yorker finds it difficult to pass one of the hundreds of schizophrenics who roam the streets without being jolted by uneasiness or fear. Oursler's figures embody the signs of mental disintegration that sometimes threaten to destabilise even the most well adjusted people. The viewer is able to relate to his babbling figures just a little too much.

Oursler sees schizophrenia encroaching on contemporary existence. As the electronic media increasingly influence one's daily experience there is accelerating confusion between television images, dream images and direct physical experience. Spewing profanity and paranoia, Oursler's figures pull the viewer into the schizophrenic mind. They embody the confusion between fantasy and reality that is already beginning to define the contemporary environment. Television has a particularly insidious effect on consciousness, in Oursler's view, inducing much of this confusion. It is not unusual for voices heard over the television set to be the first symptoms of paranoia.

The special figures in Oursler's work represent the contemporary psyche but they also refer to a long art historical tradition of visionary art. Like ambitious artists from every period of art history, Oursler is creating a model of the human condition. His dummy reciting questions from the MMPI — Minneapolis Multiphasic Personality Inventory — may be what people will look at 200 years from now to understand what it was like to be alive in 1996.'

Richard Prince: pavement pizza

'THE CRACKS at the core of American culture are not something they like to show in television. You cannot find them on the streets of a major city or even on a trip to a local shopping mall. You have to drive past the urban sprawl into the undefined areas that are not quite country but not quite suburban either; the communities that can no longer attract and hold ambitious people. This neglected part of America is not glamorous; it is not prosperous, it is not fun. It is not known to inspire art.

It has, however, inspired Richard Prince. The artist who has long been known as one of the most insightful experts on the representation of glamour [see page 144] is now wallowing in the decrepitude of exurban America. His new paintings embrace the slapped together construction, the garish colours and the sick humour that one finds in the forgotten American towns where no-one tries to impress anybody any more. The primary recreational activity is drinking, which makes most things pretty blurry by the end of the day. It does not really much matter what things look like if one cannot see them that well anyway. Prince is now entering an area where even the biker chicks would refuse to go. The sector he is studying has no trashy glamour, only trash. It is the aesthetic end of the line.

Prince's new paintings are dominated by an amorphous image resembling the back of a Barc-a-Lounger, the recliner chairs that exhausted men sit in to drink beer and watch TV. In some of the paintings, backs of heads appear, presumably attached to bodies slumped in the chairs. Beneath, or on top of the principal image, Prince has scrawled some especially sick jokes in a semi-literate script. It is the kind of handwriting you see on desperate ransom notes.

Prince's mystery image does not really need to represent anything. It may best be read as an abstraction of decrepitude, an anti-aesthetic conglomeration of clashing colours and unrelated shapes. It is a like a painter's version of a pavement pizza.

For many years, Prince's work provided insights about how people communicate on the surface. Now he seems to be burrowing deeper into the interior of the mind.' ❏

© *Excerpts by Jeffrey Deitch from* Young Americans: New American Art in the Saatchi Collection *(Saatchi, 1996)*

US DIVIDES

MARK DOW

Alien watch

News footage in April of California deputies brutally beating two Mexican immigrants, and the deaths of seven more in a car chase involving Border Patrol agents, shone a spotlight on the issue of illegal border-crossing. The US government has spent $13 million since January fortifying the border, but despite the best efforts of the Border Patrol to keep them out, nearly two million unregistered Mexicans are thought to be living in California alone

SUPERVISORY Patrol Agent Ron Grant (not his real name) is upset at what aliens are doing to his wall. 'They keep picking at our fence,' he says, showing me spots where his agents have had to patch and cement what he calls 'the famous wall'.

There are 24 miles of steel wall along the California-Mexico border, ranging from eight to 12 feet high. The longest continuous stretch is 14 miles in the San Diego Sector. But Supervisor Grant is interested only in the five to six miles of wall between San Ysidro and the Pacific Ocean. Actually, the wall doesn't stop at the Pacific: it extends 340 feet into the surf. Supervisor Grant doesn't know what is happening along the wall east of the entry point at San Ysidro and he willingly admits that he doesn't care.

The wall and the land are what he thinks about, and what he has an eye for. Then there are the aliens and his agents, acting out their roles on this set. Where there is a wall, and agents to watch the wall, fewer aliens will cross successfully. But 'even with these units', Grant tells me, the aliens are 'shameless'. 'If we stood arm to arm', he says, 'when you blinked one would get through your legs.' He laughs. 'We could use razor wire and knives' along the top of the wall, 'but that's not PC and not the American way.'

He points out a couple of obstacles that *are* allowed, what he proudly calls 'tricky little barriers'. One is a sort of rounded sheet of steel with spikes radiating from it, attached to the top of a section of wall along the dry Tijuana River channel. Another is simply a length of greased tubing along the top of the wall, on the Mexican side, which an unsuspecting alien is likely to grab onto. The wall here has been in place for about four years. Before that, it was like 'human waves', says Grant. 'You'd think it was Chinese coming at you.'

As an agent walks along the roadside looking into the brush Supervisor Grant takes a xeroxed map from his dashboard to illustrate the natural enter-chase-and-choke movement which his agents and the pursued aliens create; he makes it seem like a weather pattern happening over and over again. He talks a lot about how his men work the land to their advantage. What he resents is that they have to do everything themselves, but they do what needs to be done, whether it's building fences, bulldozing *mesas* or flattening brush. Throughout the five-hour tour we are getting out of Grant's four-wheel-drive vehicle so that he can show me the terrain up close. He wants to take me into the thick brush, where we have to bend down to follow the trails cleared by aliens. He wants me to see what an impossible job the Border Patrol has: it's hard enough to negotiate these trails by daylight and when we're not looking for anybody. He also points out the odd shoe or blanket or water bottle left behind. There is a mixture of respect and disgust in his voice when he tells me 'There's a lot of literal crawling going on for hours on end.' That's because there is a wide no-man's land to cross between the border itself and the first freeway or suburb or shopping mall.

Farther west we come to a stretch of wall that dips down into a ridge. The dip creates a blind spot on the wall for agents stationed to either side of it. Border Patrol agents, with the help of the National Guard are raising that problematic section of wall. As we approach, uniformed welders are at work, and above them, on the other side, a Mexican television cameraman approaches to film them.

We continue west to Smugglers' Canyon, where Grant points out *their* high point, a rise of land on the Mexican side of the wall. He says it's too bad we didn't accidentally bulldoze that away, adding 'Oops! Sorry.' The point is that there are things his agents have to do if they're going to

US/Mexican border, Tijuana: on the watch for aliens

accomplish their mission, which is to deter and apprehend aliens. Near Washed-Out Bridge he shows me a sandy slope that agents graded to give themselves a foothold. 'We can go down there and challenge 'em now,' he explains, 'without falling and breaking bones, and without getting up to our waists in poop water.'

Many agents keep a bottle of alcohol with them, Grant tells me, to wash off the water and blood and diseases they come in contact with. Beyond the sewage, he himself always tries to keep his hands and nails clean. He tells me this when I turn from pissing in the brush — one of the advantages of being 'a boy agent' he notes — and see that he's working on his nails. When he was trainee, he used to get kidded about this habit, because whenever he passed a pool of groundwater that had collected, he would rinse the dust off his hands. These days, the water is different. The aliens swim through sewage and they're breaking laws, he says later, in one breath.

Every little advantage counts: it's a question of who can outsmart the other. As he explains this, Grant slips and says 'agent' when he means 'alien', and laughs at the implication that the cat and the mouse are interchangeable. Which is not to say he thinks the terms of the contest are fair. On the contrary, 'we have the restrictions,' he says, 'the aliens don't.' He likens the situation to that of cops and criminals, which he knows something about. He has been in law enforcement all his adult life, beginning as a deputy sheriff in northern California almost 30 years ago. Now, as a Supervisory Border Patrol Officer, he feels he can give the agents some guidance because he's been around a while. 'We hire high-spirited people,' he says, 'then we park 'em out here.' He also has a sense of humour about the younger men (and women: 'the *hers*' are generally very good agents, he tells me as we approach the woman positioned at East High Point Lookout.) All they care about, he tells me, is their guns and ammunition. We stop near the river channel to talk to an agent who's originally from Minnesota, where he worked in a bakery, then earned a degree in political science. He took the exams for federal jobs, and the first offer was from the Border Patrol. He asks where my article will appear, and Grant interrupts: if it's not in *Soldier of Fortune*, *Guns & Ammo* or *Penthouse*, he laughs, these guys won't see it.

Grant wants me to know that when he was a young Border Patrol agent, he had a them–against–us view of things, and he loved the chase. Now, he says, he has a mellower attitude towards immigration. He hopes he can pass some of that attitude along to the agents he supervises, but he also feels he has to keep his personal feelings separate from his job. He is also concerned about his agents' morale. He explains the difference between 'morale boosters' and 'morale busters'. One booster was transferring aliens all the way to El Paso before they were returned to Mexico. A buster is announced at the briefing for the incoming shift: since the holding facility at El Centro is full, agents must 'turn everybody [apprehended] loose with a piece of paper,' except those known as 'criminal aliens'.

Then there are the environmentalists. Grant refers to them as 'the burnt-turtle people' because they were worried about the potential harm to some turtles if the Border Patrol went forward with plans to burn off some of the low brush which aliens use for cover. The burnt-turtle people also complain about our agents stepping on endangered species' nests and eggs' but do they complain about the aliens trampling on them? At the Imperial Beach Station, there are photos and descriptions of terns and their nests and eggs tacked up on the bulletin board.

Knowing that they, and not the aliens, face the obstacles 'demoralis[es] the troops', Grant complains. On one side is the 'aggressive alien', he continues, and on the other side are his agents, choking on dust and pollen, subject to the 'threat of physical attack'. When I ask about incidents in which agents have been attacked, he admits he can't think of any in particular. Back near the entry point at San Ysidro, he had pointed out a narrow gravel road between the river channel and a grassy slope, and told me it's called 'memo lane'. As a result of fights and having to take aliens into physical custody, he explains somewhat elliptically, agents working that stretch tend to write a lot of memos.

Human Rights Watch/Americas and the American Friends Service Committee's Mexico-US Border Program have documented numerous abuses by the Border Patrol over the years. Grant refers to such groups as 'our detractors', and is angry that they can shoot off their mouths with no proof of their charges, and still get on the front pages of the 'fish-wrap newspapers'. At the Imperial Beach Station, videos are playing for aliens in holding cells awaiting return. Actually, the video we stop to watch is playing in front of an empty cell; the bracket for a monitor in the crowded cell next to it has no TV. We watch a tape of the Border Patrol's rescue operation for aliens in a flooding Tijuana River. 'I bet he's glad to have that cup of coffee,' says Grant. Then we see some text scroll by, starting with the words 'Si tiene ud denuncios' — 'if you have any complaint...' This time Grant doesn't even laugh. He just says, '"Hi, I'm Ron, your Border Patrol agent. If I hit you too hard, here's a number to call"'... We've done everything but put an ACLU office in our office.'

Grant and another agent process an alien and show me their computer system. Instead of using the old-fashioned ink, they have the alien put his finger on an electronic pad, and his print appears on the screen. Next time, if he uses an alias, that will simply get filed along with his print. The various databases the Immigration and Naturalization Service (INS) use to identify aliens and others are not linked up nationwide yet. 'Compartmentalisation [is] the American way,' says Grant, 'so we're not a police state.' But, he smiles, he wouldn't mind if we were, 'since I'm the police.' He gestures towards a surveillance camera mounted on the ceiling.

Saying it monitors everything that goes on in the station, he starts talking about accusations from his detractors again. Maybe there is 'an unjust thump' sometimes, he admits, but what do you expect? That's 'human nature'. Imagine that you're 'up there surrounded by 1,500 aliens'. They have their bonfires (earlier he had pointed to a charred area on the Mexican side of the wall, where aliens gather and cook, keep warm and wait.) You're defensive, you're scared, 'and suddenly they're here in your country — what would you, the general population, do?' That's when he adds, they swim through sewage, they're breaking the laws. 'This [station] is not the Fontainebleau in Miami.' An agent is moving the aliens from the cell on to a bus just outside the door. Grant points to boxes of juice and cookies in the processing area for the women and children who are apprehended. Still, there's 'no end' to the nice things we do for them, he says: 'that's our nice side.'

Supervisor Grant may not have mixed feelings about the wall, but he does feel it's a shame it has to exist. Because he worked for three years as the INS attaché in the US Consulate in Mexico City, he says he has a different view from many of his colleagues. On the one hand, there are 'those wonderful people' in Mexico; on the other hand, there are 'the poor, illiterate and unsavoury' ones crossing here illegally. I ask him what he thinks would happen after a few days if there were no wall and no Border Patrol. At first he jokes that it would be a vacuum cleaner or a flushing toilet — though 'the former sounds better to our detractors.' Then he says seriously, 'I don't know,' and speculates that the flow might find its own level; it's like drug legalisation, he observes, in that we can't know without trying it. But he also says the wall is necessary as long as we're dealing with 'a high-risk country that might put us out of business': places like Pakistan, the Philippines — or Mexico. His position is that his job is to carry out policies devised in Washington. For the time being, under the Clinton administration, things are happening, meaning that more funds are coming to his agency. And that translates into more agents and more vehicles with which to get the job done.

But Grant also observes that both the Mexicans and the Americans are ambivalent about immigration. The Mexicans look at the Border Patrol the way we look at the IRS. They demonise us with no rationale, he says; they want to be like us, but they hate us. As for Americans, they all want to do something about illegal immigrants, except the one working for them. The Democrats are bleeding hearts, he continues, and the

Republicans want 'slaves for their corporate farms'. Then he tells me something about himself.

A PhD who once spoke at a Border Patrol training session said that we all have 'significant emotional experiences' that make lasting impressions on us. When he was a boy, Grant says, up in Fresno County, he was working four jobs — including the post office, a gas station, and a car dealership. His parents were 'farmworkers' — he changes this to 'fieldworkers'. His father had come to California from Indiana; his grandfather was from Topeka. His mother was Mexican, from the state of Chihuahua. When I ask, he smiles and says he doesn't know if she was legal or not. Anyway, he developed a cyst on his tailbone, and every so often the doctor would lance it and drain the pus. Eventually the doctor told him the cyst had to be removed, but he couldn't afford to go to a private hospital. So he went to the 'county hospital', not knowing what that meant, though now he understands it was for indigents. As a boy, he just saw it as the hospital for Hispanics and Blacks and 'what we used to call Okies, in other words, poor whites'. So he went to the county hospital, and there he was told he did not qualify; he didn't understand why. He was 10 years old. That was one of his 'significant emotional experiences'. 'I became a Republican Nazi Gestapo Conservative,' he says. Years later, when asked why he voted for Reagan, 'I said, "because Hitler wasn't running".'

At Smugglers' Canyon, there is a break in the wall because a steep crevice makes construction too difficult. Several young Mexican men are standing there, on the other side, watching us. We stop to talk with them. The conversation begins sarcastically, with Grant asking (in Spanish) if they're waiting until it gets dark before they cross. All of them are silent except one. He's wearing a 'D.A.R.E. TO KEEP KIDS OFF DRUGS' T-shirt. He asks Grant if he'd mind taking a look at his papers. The two of them have difficulty negotiating the end of the wall because of that steep crevice. So the Mexican disappears for a moment, then comes through a hole in the wall and sits on a rock in the United States, while Supervisor Grant looks at his documents. These turn out to be a photo ID card from a factory in Escondido, just north of San Diego, and a pay stub from the week before. Grant asks him why he is crossing *de pollo* — like a chicken, as the expression goes — if he has a job. The Mexican answers that he was picked up recently and returned. In other words, he hasn't been working here legally. His wife, however, *is* here legally, and so are their children. He didn't know that this gives him the possibility of being here legally, too. So Grant explains the application process to him. As we're leaving, Grant tells him, you do your job and cross, and I'll do mine and bring you back. Then he adds, wait until after three o'clock when my shift is over, so I'm not the one to catch you. The Mexican nods and goes back through the wall.

Grant wants me to see that the chased and the chasers share an understanding. 'Our detractors' accuse the agency of being racist, but how can an agency that's 40-50 per cent Hispanic be racist? As for the in-house ethnic jokes, there's a certain type of humour that's common in law enforcement; it's what keeps us going, and if the ACLU-PC crowd doesn't think it's funny, too bad for them. I ask him if he's noticed whether any of his Hispanic agents have conflicts about doing their job. They don't, he responds, because when we're doing our job, we all know that 'it's Americans catching Mexicans.'

Back at the station, Grant hoses the dust off his official vehicle, and we switch to his personal vehicle so that he can drop me at the trolley station. Tucked between the bucket seats is a small, hardwood baseball bat — *Hecho en México* — that his son bought him for 10 pesos (about US$3); 'having been in a few scrapes, I'm not averse to a game of baseball'. He puts on a flannel shirt over his uniform shirt, because he doesn't want to get pulled into some couple's domestic argument while he's waiting at a stoplight on his way home. He has lived nearby, in a suburb of San Diego, for years. Back near the wall, he's been noticing some wild hydrangeas recently. He likes their bright colours, and he's thinking of collecting some of the seeds one of these days to plant in his backyard. ❏

Mark Dow is a freelance writer based in Miami, Florida

Further reading: Human Rights Watch/Americas: *Crossing the Line: Human Rights Abuses Along the US Border with Mexico Persist Amid Climate of Impunity* (New York, April 1995); *Frontier Injustice: Human Rights Abuses Along the US Border with Mexico Persist Amid Climate of Impunity* (13 May, 1993); and American Friends Service Committee Immigration Law Enforcement Monitoring Project: *Women at the US-Mexico Border: Violation of Women's Rights as Human Rights in Border Crossings* (Houston, September 1995); *Sealing Our Borders: The Human Toll* (Philadelphia, February 1992)

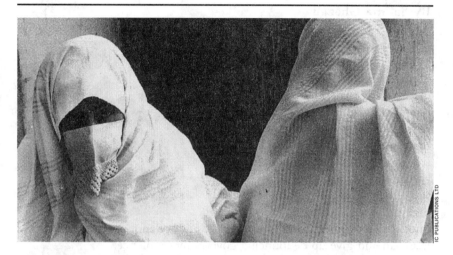

IC PUBLICATIONS LTD

Algeria: a dossier from inside

The publication by a group of human rights lawyers of the details of a prison massacre concealed by the authorities for over a year, could be a turning point in breaking the silence that has surrounded government atrocities and the fate of the many dead and 'disappeared' victims of Algeria's civil war. On 4 March, *La Nation*, one of the few remaining independent weeklies, followed this up with the first human rights dossier to dwell on government — as opposed to Islamist — atrocities. The issue was not published in Algeria, but in France, *Le Monde Diplomatique* published it in full. *Index* publishes for the first time in English, excerpts from the dossier as well as an interview with its editor, Salima Ghezali (see page 100)

Citizenship *v* barbarism

By Salima Ghezali

'You can't fight terrorism in kid gloves with the declaration of human rights in your hand.' For a great many of Algeria's politicians this dictum has become the excuse for not examining too closely the state's repression of the Islamist movement and its surrender to ignorance and barbarism. Any attempt at dialogue stumbles on this unavoidable precondition: to join the club of 'modernisers' and 'patriots' you must set about denouncing terrorism and Islamism and give up denouncing government violence.

Islamist terrorism is clearly one form of barbarism. The unleashing of violence in Algeria is mainly the result of a conception of conflict where any means, even the most appalling, are justified to win power. The suffering and injuries Algerians have experienced at the hands of the Islamists have split society open, and it will take a long time to repair the damage. But this split is equally the result of a policy of massive repression and of a 'modernism' whose defence of authoritarian privileges exhausts and abuses democracy's intellectual armoury. The methods of the two belligerents are often equally ferocious. Between these two camps, a gagged population suffers the full force of every type of terror and is constantly urged to take sides to eliminate, physically and without compassion, the 'enemy'.

This battlefield logic fosters secular bigotry, stirs up old rivalries and tribalism and thrives on the fears fed by propaganda. The brief experience of pluralism between 1989 and 1991 was not long enough to develop a responsive democracy. As a result, discussion of human rights is treated with scepticism: a convenient bolt-hole for all sides. The situation is aggravated by the behaviour of the governing party, whose control of the media during their long decades in power created a passive population, indifferent to news. Television, even more than the press, acts as part of the war machine, inventing stories or avoiding issues as the state commands.

Every day the gap grows between those blinded by state propaganda and the Islamists who are encouraged in their brutal rebellion by the others' indifference to their suffering. When laws are made solely to restrict freedom, as the recent security information act confirms, it becomes difficult to appeal for respect for the law. In such an atmosphere the policies set out by the main opposition parties — the National Liberation Front (FLN), the Islamic Salvation Front (FIS) and the Socialist Forces Front (FFS) — in Rome in January 1995 denouncing all violence and appealing for respect for the various international human rights treaties, represented a real step forward.

Affirming the principle of the inviolability of the person is the triumph of reason over hysteria and fear. In recognising an opponent's humanity, the true democrat restores to man what fanaticism and despotism deny: the right to dignity. Radicals of both camps regularly use their enemy's ideology to justify their own shortcomings as they slide into bloodshed.

In the Algerian tragedy, the terrorists' despicable violence, with its trail of mutilated bodies and booby-trapped car-bombs — the most appalling of which killed 42 and injured 286 on 30 January 1995 in front of the main Algiers police station — is often and rightly recalled. But why is there almost total silence about the violent way order is restored? Human rights organisations like Amnesty International and Human Rights Watch repeatedly protest against the abuses committed by both sides.

Some human rights organisations have come up against a serious dilemma. Shocked by the horror of terrorism as much as by the extremism of the Islamists' rhetoric, activists have questioned whether the same humanitarian standards should be applied to the terrorists. Such an attitude, if it became widespread, would be an unexpected ally of both religious fundamentalism and government violence. States freed from the healthy pressure put on them by human rights groups would be unlikely to encounter any resistance to their plan to subjugate individuals. Whether in power or in opposition, the fundamentalists, who claim that there are no universal human rights principles, would be strengthened.

The passivity of democrats towards the abuses of which they are the victims is cited by some Islamists as proof that universal principles applying equally to all do not exist. The most radical take advantage of this to stir up young people disaffected by the innumerable unreported injustices they suffer, while a big fuss is made about violence inflicted on other social groups. Shut out from society, the extremist becomes an isolated being on the path to a martyrdom which he will force on his victims, confident that no principle nor tie bonds humanity across its differences.

One can find experts to dwell at length on the character of such and such an ideology, but anyone can see that the more violent the regime the more radical the opposition. Faced with the rise of extremism and the unleashing of hysteria, remembering the principles on which the human community is founded and watchfulness — toward state terror as much as toward that of the paramilitaries — are the best means to ensure that citizenship defeats barbarism.

Massacre at Serkadji

NEWSPAPERS published the story of the massacre at Serkadji in their morning editions of 22 February 1995. They spoke of an 'attempted breakout' allegedly on 'the previous evening'. Next day, they reported that the riot had been put down.

Over the next few days, the press played the story down, attempting to dismiss suspicions that anything untoward or unusual had happened. But it's not easy to conceal the massacre of a hundred or so in the state's keeping, especially since this was not the first time there had been a massacre in a state prison: in November 1994, prisoners — their number still unknown — were killed in Berrouaghia Prison, east of Algiers.

The families of victims and witnesses were convinced that this monstrous attack had been designed to liquidate prisoners. That the state itself could do this, 'was every bit as terrifying as the fear instilled by the terrorists'.

The government enquiry, set up on 27 February 1995 under the minister of the interior Abderrahmane Meziane Cherif, has still not made its findings public; nor has the government published a list of victims nor acted to ensure the preservation of material evidence in the case. Televised confessions supporting the official version of events have been extracted under torture.

Painstakingly and with great courage, a lawyers' group pieced together a preliminary report on the killing at Serkadji. Compiled at the request of the families of victims, their document throws light on events the authorities have done their best to keep under wraps.

The lawyers' report not only draws attention to the as yet unexplained behaviour of the authorities, but also details efforts made by prisoners to contact the authorities and work out a peaceful solution. Despite which, the authorities resorted to force: the official death toll is 96 plus 10 wounded. Witnesses in the report speak of 'a butchery' beyond words. 'The remains of the victims, or what was left of them, were taken to the morgue at Bologhine in plastic rubbish sacks. They were left there in a heap for several days and allowed to rot.'

Relatives were left in suspense, their agony compounded by the burial of the majority of prisoners in secret graves marked only with the rubric: 'X, Algerian'. And 'when they were given the number of a grave, it was selected at random without any indication, nor means of finding out, who was really buried in a particular spot.'

Abridged version of the article by Salima Ghezali in La Nation*'s dossier*

Graveyards of the unknown dead

By Lakhdar Benyounes

ALGERIA is haunted by the ghostly voices of its disappeared, those who never came home. To the courts these are 'unsolved cases'; memory says otherwise.

The gravediggers know everything. Those who died in Serkadji? Go straight ahead, past the great cypresses that enclose the former boundary of the state cemetery of El Alia. All the workers here know the macabre fascination this spot holds, but, out of caution, ask no questions.

As they have done for so many who come here, they simply point the way and bend once more to their digging.

To get here, you have to cross the cemetery from end to end. First, the area reserved for state burials where history has gathered Algeria's heroes of past and present, friends and enemies alike. Then past the small space reserved for Christian graves, some of which are by now almost a century old. Almost immediately, you arrive at an immense area downstream from the old fortress, overflowing with the swelling ranks of the dead. Even though today is not Friday, the day Muslims visit the graves, a group of women is already here, silently weeding and tidying up the graves that have been battered by last night's rains.

Each has lost a husband, a father, a brother. Each has, at least, the sad satisfaction of knowing where their loved ones are buried. The names are daubed in paint, sometimes simply scrawled in marker pen on the graves: Djebbour Abderrahman, killed 16 December 1995; Chehilat Kouider, murdered 16 January 1994; Lounici Sallah, died 2 March 1993... Bad enough. But luckier than those who are tending the unnamed dead, the endless ranks of anonymous graves in this part of the cemetery. 'Lots of folk come searching. They poke around, find nothing,' says one of the workers. 'There's no saying if they'll ever find what they're looking for.'

Alongside the orderly rows of old gravestones, the new graves are all over the place. The terrain looks like a vast building site: the graves cheek by jowl in the mud; no attempt at order or identification. They cover an area hundreds of metres square; many among them are neglected, overgrown and without the flowers customary on Algerian graves.

Some of the prisoners killed in the prison mutiny are buried here. Some are identifiable and seem to have been visited regularly. Others are marked only by a number or semi-legible character. Others again, disowned even by death, unknown and untended, are already disappearing beneath the weight of the earth and the rain. An aged worker tells us these corpses are often brought here at the end of the afternoon, in rough wooden coffins. No-one knows what they contain.

Where do they come from? Given that the residents of Sidi Moussa and Khémis El Khechna are confronted daily with corpses on their streets and that here, as in other suburbs of the town, they are constantly stumbling over bodies, it's a meaningless question. But the old man proffers an answer: 'Those who were killed in Serkadji certainly, but also those who have been decapitated and their bodies picked up off the streets. Last Tuesday,' he relates, 'an ambulance arrives. The ambulancemen bury someone, fill in the grave and drive off. After all, the dead must be buried,' he concludes with grisly logic.

The scene is repeated in other cemeteries; jumbled graves, unmarked, half hidden and impossible to find without the all-knowing gravediggers. A lawyer representing the family of a victim speaks with conviction of 'mass graves' where bodies have been buried 'while they were still warm'.

Between two fires

By Ghania Mouffok

A FTER four years of being reigned in, the new shape of the media reflects the new political map drawn up after the 16 November 1995 presidential election reckoned finally to have put to rest the parliamentary elections of 1991 [see *Index* 4&5/1994; 3/1995].

In a word: as far as those in power are concerned, the role of the media is to form national and international opinion in favour of the workings of a regime that is a past master in the art of manipulating the facts.

With only their skills as writers to call on, those journalists who continue to write for the independent press despite fear of intimidation and the deaths of their colleagues play the role of a paper forum. In the absence of any democratic institutions, it is they who publish and discuss the policies and press releases of the parties and government; of the unions and of ordinary citizens. Last witness to a disappearing democracy, the independent press is also the barometer of its health. The way in which it is treated by the authorities indicates which way the winds of free expression and other rights in Algeria will blow.

Developments since the election of Liamine Zeroual leave little room for optimism: imprisonments, assassinations, strikes and censorship prove the nightmare is not over.

And there are other problems. Since the government announced forthcoming increases in printing costs, the debate on whether or not the independent press should cut a 'political deal' has taken over front pages. The private press is wholly dependent on state-owned printing houses and, since the government can no longer afford to write off their chronic deficit, it seems likely that market prices will be the death of several titles — for whom, in any case, an ungrateful government has little further use.

Contrary to the views of many commentators we are not simply marking time. In the words of one such, 'We are back in 1965. Dictatorship has returned, but this time without any vision other than staying in power.' ❑

Dossier compiled by the staff of La Nation. *These excerpts translated by Judith Vidal-Hall and Nicholas McAulay. The complete dossier will be published on our World Wide Web site at http://www.oneworld.org/index_oc/*

REVIEW

JULIAN PETLEY

SALLY OLDING

It may be hi-tech, 't ain't sense

Quick-fix technical answers to complex social problems only compound the issues they seek to resolve

THE v-chip seems at first sight to be the answer to every concerned parent's prayers; a device that will enable them to stop their offspring watching unsuitable TV programmes. The idea has some powerful supporters. In the USA, President Clinton has signed the

Telecommunications Bill, making it compulsory for all new televisions to be fitted with the chip from 1998; the European Parliament has passed a similar amendment to the Television Without Frontiers directive; and UK heritage secretary Virginia Bottomley, under pressure from Liberal Democrat MP David Alton has ordered an enquiry into introducing the chip into British televisions.

The v-chip, however, is a purely technological response to what is essentially a social and regulatory problem. Namely, how do we protect children from potentially disturbing images whilst respecting the rights of adults to watch material which is not suitable for children? And like all such responses, the more one examines its practical aspects, the more it seems like a quick fix whose benefits are largely illusory and consequences probably undesirable.

First, the chip will be most used by parents who already regulate their children's viewing. The availability of a new gizmo is not going to turn irresponsible parents into responsible ones. Furthermore, the ratings system on which the v-chip depends risks creating the lure of 'forbidden fruit', and children from strictly regulated homes are likely to gather to watch adult-rated programmes at the homes of friends whose parents are less regulation-minded. It is also entirely possible that, given children's ease with modern technology, and many parents' complete inability even to programme a video recorder, the former will simply find ways to circumvent the chip. And finally, on the subject of children, whilst people are right to be concerned that some children are needlessly disturbed by being allowed to watch unsuitable programmes by careless parents, what of the children of over-protective parents? Do we really want to make it any easier for them to grow up with a blinkered and unrealistic view of the world? Adult responsibility for children's exposure to the media is not going to be fulfilled by programming a mechanical device; children need to be talked with about what they see on television, especially if it's problematic. And this is the responsibility not only of parents but of properly informed teachers as well.

As far as adult viewing is concerned, there is a danger that the v-chip could backfire in the face of its supporters such as David Alton. After all, if children really could be stopped from seeing unsuitable programmes then there would be a convincing argument for allowing adults to see 'stronger' ones than they can at present. This is the argument currently used by some of the satellite channels in the case of their encrypted services. Is this what Alton and Co want? Hardly, I would suggest. No wonder, then, that Mary Whitehouse, founding former head of the moral watchdog, the National Viewers' and Listeners' Association, is against the chip, arguing that 'all broadcasters in Britain have an obligation not to transmit programmes that offend against taste and decency. The v-chip puts all the responsibility onto parents, which is neither realistic nor fair.' In these circumstances, one wonders what the proponents of ever-tougher censorship, for that is what they are, will come up with next.

Furthermore, who is going to work out the ratings on which the effectiveness of the v-chip will depend? What will be needed will be a classification system similar to that currently operated by the British Board of Film Classification (BBFC). Thus, for example, a parent could set the v-chip to block all programmes rated higher than PG or, alternatively, could work on a programme-by-programme basis to screen out what they considered unsuitable. This, of course, would depend on the availability of reliable information about programmes; the problem is, of course, that judgements could well be made on the basis of lurid and inaccurate press accounts of programmes. And what kind of vast and costly bureaucracy is going to work out the ratings system? Will the BBC, Independent Television Commission (ITC), Broadcasting Standards Council (BSC) and the satellite broadcasters ever be able to work out common standards? If the EU does introduce the chip, will there have to be European-wide standards? This should be fun, since most of the UK's continental neighbours have far more liberal standards on screen sex and violence than Britain. Cue floods of 'alien porn' stories from the Europhobic press.

On the surface, classification always seems like a sensible idea, a form of consumer advice which helps viewers to avoid material which they may not want to see, or their children to see. The problem, however, is that it's almost impossible to devise a system which is objective and isn't coloured by the classifiers' moral judgement. Now there is, of course, nothing remotely wrong in moral judgement per se, but as a basis for classification — and, where it is felt necessary, censorship — it does raise some fundamental questions. For example, should all art be 'moral', as Miss Prism thought it should? Can or should one trust the moral judgement of the classifiers? Is it possible or desirable, in a diverse and heterodox society such as ours, to abrogate moral judgement to a central classifying body? As the twentieth century draws to a close, shouldn't we at last be considered grown-up enough to make our own moral judgements?

Anybody who believes that classification is a simple, 'objective' matter should look at the 1994-95 annual report of the BBFC, a document in the best tradition of Miss Prism, Dr Bowdler and Charles Lamb. So, for example, cuts for the Schwarzenegger film *True Lies* because of 'glamorous, eye-catching ferocity by the role-model himself' but thumbs up to *Reservoir Dogs* since 'the characters suffer for their indulgence in violence, and crime is rarely seen to pay...morally the film is unproblematic'; to *The Good Son*, a film with a 'strong moral core'; and to *Shopping*, for which the BBFC actually called in the police, who advised them that 'the film had been careful not to show any imitable techniques of joy-riding or ram-raiding, and they agreed that, far from profiting from their misdeeds, the protagonists were seen to perish without ever achieving much success as role models.' Nor is the BBFC in the least averse to passing such airy judgements as 'heroes at "15" must be acceptable role models and should not match the brutality of their opponents blow for blow', or 'cinema tends to glamorise whatever it shows, even when aiming for the truth.' Well, personally I didn't find Auschwitz, or Nazism, glamorous in *Schindler's List*, but perhaps I'm odd. And, talking of concentration camps, the report whips itself up into such a frenzy of hysteria over two mild, soft-core, women-in-prison films

SALLY OLDING

which it rejected, that its lurid accounts of them bear little relation to the films themselves. To read this purple prose, with its talk of 'peaks of evil or atrocity', one really would think that one was dealing with sadistic hard-core pornography of the worst kind, not elderly, rather campy, tongue-in-cheek productions which are freely available elsewhere in the world. If anything underlined my earlier point about the difficulty of making classificatory judgements with which others could agree, then this opinionated, over-heated fricassee of exaggeration and moral outrage, larded with references to 'American research' — which is nothing like as authoritative as the BBFC would have us believe — is surely it.

Of course, one could defend the BBFC by arguing that it had highly questionable legislation imposed upon it in the wake of unfounded press reports of the role allegedly played by *Child's Play 3* in the murders of James Bulger and Suzanne Capper (*Index* 1/1995). This requires the BBFC to have 'special regard...to any harm that may be caused to potential viewers or, through their behaviour, to society by the manner in which the work deals with: — criminal behaviour, illegal drugs, violent behaviour or incidents, horrific behaviour or incidents, or human sexual activity.' However, the report itself makes such a defence impossible since, as it explains, 'these criteria represent not a break with former policy, but a confirmation of it, since they put on the face of the legislation factors which the Board has been taking into account for many years.' Nonetheless, it cannot be emphasised too strongly that the notion of images doing 'harm' (or, for that matter, good) to viewers is highly contentious; one that rests on a particularly crude, mechanistic and behaviourist way of conceptualising the relationship between images and audiences, and which is simply not accepted by the majority of media researchers in this country. This is not, as it is often caricatured as being, the same thing as saying that media have no influence whatsoever on people. It is, however, extremely disturbing that film and video censorship in the UK is based on a model of human behaviour and a conception of media 'effects' that are, to put it mildly, highly dubious and questionable. Were they to be adopted as the basis for the classification of television programmes they would have to be fought tooth and nail. ❑

Julian Petley is head of Communication and Information Studies at Brunel University, UK

Index online

The **INDEX** website on the Internet is already attracting over 25,000 visitors a month. In March, it was shortlisted for the **MEDIA NATURA AWARDS**, and in April it was awarded five stars by the **BEST OF THE PLANET** awards website (http://www.2ask.com/BOTP/5star.html)

The Internet allows us to supplement the in-depth coverage and analysis in the magazine. Features on the site include:

• regular reports from our Africa editor, Adewale Maja-Pearce, in Lagos
• a gallery of banned cartoons from 25 countries
• for those with audio technology, the voice of Frank Ortega telling the story of Chinese human rights activist Wei Jingsheng

The Internet has the potential to give free speech a massive boost. Inevitably, it also provides the censor with new opportunities for control and suppression. At *Index* we're keeping a very close eye on developments. Our website is a way of gathering news as well as distributing it. Through it we aim to promote interactive debate on censorship issues, as well as providing a new resource for users.

**I keep finding stories [on your website] which emerge from *Index* which I wish I'd known about before.
Vivienne Walt, *Wall Street Journal***

Since many of our readers in the developing world do not yet have access to the technology which will enable them to use the World Wide Web itself economically, we are working with GreenNet to establish text-only conferences to allow them to join us.

So to see the latest censorship news, and to give us your own news and comments, go to:

INDEX *online*
http://www.oneworld.org/index_oc/

LETTER FROM LAGOS

ADEWALE MAJA-PEARCE

Once more unto the polls...

Votes come cheap in Nigeria's latest flirtation with democracy

NIGERIANS are a fickle people who don't deserve democracy and probably won't get it. Barely three years after the annulment of the June 1993 elections, and with the presumed winner still in detention on charges of treason, the would-be citizens of this vast and troublesome nation obligingly trooped off to designated centres on successive Saturdays in March (16 and 23) to vote in local council elections as part of yet another transition to civil rule. The entire transition programme itself, which was unveiled late last year, is scheduled to culminate in October 1998, whereupon General Sani Abacha, the latest incarnation of military rule that has plagued this country since decolonisation in 1960, will apparently hand over to an elected civilian president, and Nigeria, the 'giant of Africa', will once more assume its honoured place among the comity of nations (or words to that effect).

The local council elections were held on a 'zero–party basis', ostensibly in recognition of Nigeria's 'historical and cultural peculiarities', but in reality to enable the government to interfere at will without raising charges of political favouritism. In one state alone, 100 prospective delegates previously cleared by the National Electoral Commission were summarily banned after 'further screening carried out by the state security agents' on the very morning that voting was to take place. The government naturally denied that it was intent on packing the councils with its surrogates, but any debate about the matter was in any case academic. Section 45 of the Local Government Decree 6 of 1996 empowers the Head of State to remove any councillor 'found to be compromising his non-partisan political standing', a piece of gobbledygook which, insofar as it means anything at all, can only mean what the Head of State wants it to mean. Additionally, Section 12 of the same decree ousts the jurisdiction of the courts in all matters relating to the elections. The Head of State giveth and the Head of State taketh away...

The government, of course, was absolutely delighted with the 'massive turnout', as one respected newspaper put it (*The Guardian on Sunday*, 17 March), and a jubilant Dr Walter Ofonagoro, the minister for information and culture spoke the truth for once when he declared that 'Abacha's regime has been vindicated' by this show of numbers, estimated at up to 24 million people. Various imported observers from the USA who nobody except the government had ever heard of before, but who were nevertheless privileged to observe the sad spectacle from the air-conditioned comfort of their chauffeur-driven limousines (who said that Nigeria was a poor country?), promised to relay the good news to President Clinton in order that he might stop once and for all any further talk of sanctions and freezing the assets of military officers. According to the statement issued by their spokesperson: 'I saw the eagerness of the people to vote... I think they should be encouraged.'

The Nigerian intelligentsia, for their part, revealed once again their limitless capacity for self-delusion when the facts on the ground refuse to conform to their sentimental pretences concerning the behaviour of their wayward compatriots. An editorial in *ThisDay*, another respected newspaper of impeccable liberal credentials, contrived to interpret the entire charade as a 'vote for democracy' ('The message in the large turnout of voters was clear and unmistaken: that the people of Nigeria are set and ready for democracy'); and the reverend Matthew Hassan Kukah of the Catholic Secretariat, who, it seems, is never out of the limelight these days pronouncing on every twist and turn in what Wole Soyinka once termed 'the nation's political pathology', substituted emotive language for reasoned argument in his determination to prove that two and two came to anything but four:

> The real issue to my mind is that Nigerian people are ready to come out at the sound of any voice that trumpets the democratic call. That is why hungry, thirsty, fed up, traumatised, humiliated, yet our people are still determined to assert their democratic rights for what they are worth. (*ThisDay*, 29 March)

As fantasies go, this is as dangerous as the notion that the military is capable of midwifing democracy (to use its own terminology) even as it continues to incarcerate journalists and human rights activists whose only crime is to have called for the realisation of that democracy in the shortest possible time; but why a people yearning to be free couldn't simply have used their most effective weapon and stayed at home in protest was understood clearly enough by the aspiring politicians currently jostling for their share of the nation's spoils. Completely devoid as they are of patriotism, and knowing only too well which way 'our people' will always jump when the military cracks the whip, the would-be guardians of civil rule simply gave their compatriots what they knew they wanted:

> The amount is N200 (£1.50),' said one voter, gleefully showing his wad of banknotes. 'During the last election I did not get any money, but this time I must get something. I am here with my wife, my sister-in-law and her two friends. Between five of us we are getting N1,000 today. (*The Guardian*, 19 March)

This particular voter and his retinue were at least fortunate enough to be living in Lagos, the commercial capital. Five naira was apparently enough in some parts of the country to get the 'hungry, thirsty, fed up, traumatised, humiliated' to sell their birthright, but what to do? Any self-avowed democrat is bound to respect the collective will of the Nigerian people and never mind how deplorable one might find the expression of that collective will to be. The fact that the Nigerian people have themselves voluntarily acceded to the annulment of the 1993 elections, and with it any hope of the 'enduring democracy' that the Abacha regime never tires of promising to deliver even as it does everything to ensure that no such beast emerges in the near future, only suggests a shabby collusion between the rulers and the ruled that can hardly be gainsaid by the wishful thinking of those who yearn for the giant of Africa to assume its honoured place, etc etc. ❑